I Think Therefore I Am Wrong

A Guide to Bias, Political Correctness, Fake News and the Future of Mankind

Howard J. Rankin PhD

Cover design by Barbara Morello-O'Donnell. Cover photo by Denis Dove.

Table of Contents

Introduction

The holter monitor I had been wearing showed that a few hours had elapsed since I had first put it on. I was wearing it as part of a cardiovascular assessment and tomorrow, first thing, I would go on my typical run, so that my heart rate could be recorded during aerobic exercise before turning the device back in to the clinic.

I woke up at six and saw that the monitor now had a blank screen. Where there had been elapsed time showing, now there was nothing.

"Shoot!" I said to myself. "What a drag. Well, there's no point going for that run now," I said to myself laying back down on the bed.

I ruminated about the technician who had set the holter monitor up. I knew he was new to the position because I saw that he was getting coaching from one of the other nurses as he was helping the person in front of me.

"I thought he only replaced one of the batteries," I recalled. Obviously he didn't replace all of them.

"Damn. Well, I'm not going through all this again," I said to myself, frustration beginning to mount.

"You would think that a physician's office would make sure that stuff like this doesn't happen. And a cardiologist of all people! This could be stressful. Someone in worse shape than I might have had a heart attack, for heaven's sake." The thoughts kept on coming, piling on top of each other in a veritable mound of cards.

For the next hour or so before I got back to the cardiologist, I planned out what I was going to say. I understand that the technician is a rookie and sure we all make mistakes. Still, I would convey my frustration but not in any vindictive way. Don't be too hard on him. Don't want to get the guy fired, he's just learning.

On the way, to the cardiologist I practiced my speech to the doctor. "Not to worry, these things happen," I will say cheerfully, covering my frustration that only had been building for the last hour and a half, despite my best intentions.

I walked into the cardiologist's office and handed the receptionist my monitor.

"I think it's stopped working," I said as I handed it over. "The screen is blank."

The receptionist checked it out.

"No, it's working. It's fine," she said.

Ever since I had woken up I had been the victim of my own thought process. I must have inadvertently turned off the screen at some point and not realized. Then I did what we are prone to do, assume that it was someone else's fault.

We have all been there and experienced it because our thinking process is far from perfect. In fact, it is flawed. We may have been given the gift of rationality but it is not how we think. We are storytellers, with imperfect perception, erroneous memory and a need to feel in control at all costs. And that process defines much of what we call "thinking."

Our faulty thinking stems from our perceptions and beliefs that lead us to making false assumptions and more. In the example above, my thought process was quite sane and logical *once I assumed the holter monitor wasn't working.* But our thought process leads to us jumping to false conclusions and after that, it doesn't matter how rational you are, you're on the fast track to nowhere good. If I think the lamp is talking to me and telling me to do satanic things, it is perfectly rational for me to unplug it. Logic is simply a system of deductions *once you have an assumption*. But the core issue is where do the assumptions come from?

Moreover, if I had mentioned to anyone my opinions of the trainee technician, I would have been spreading fake news, even though I was convinced I was right.

This real life example of my experience with the holter monitor is in many ways trivial even if it is illustrative. But the same process that led me astray can result in vindictive actions, slanderous judgments, and hurtful beliefs not just of others but ourselves, too. It can lead to divorces, wars and eons of false beliefs and misunderstandings. And pseudoscience. And fake news.

And it will influence the future of mankind.

Our mental process hardly ever stops. It churns on and on, relentlessly generating thoughts, beliefs and judgments, most of which are false at worst and partially true at best. Even our more accurate moments are over-simplified versions of reality that miss important aspects of the truth. And the endless stream of consciousness might not just be part of our experience, it might actually detract from a full experience of who we are and how to appreciate life. As we shall see, that endless chatter in your head might not serve any good purpose. You might just be rubbernecking your way through life distracted by shiny objects that hook you in and not only waste your time and energy but hijack your identity.

In the days before modern technology and social media, there wasn't much for people to do in their spare time. Instead of playing brain expanding games like Candy Crush and making crucial social connections on Facebook, people had to talk to each other about things like, "What is reality?" and "What are beliefs?" and "Is knowledge even possible?"

One of these presumably bored guys was the 17th century philosopher Descartes who famously said, "I think, therefore I am." Descartes is part of a long tradition of philosophers who tried to work out what truth and knowledge really mean and if they can even be attained.

For Descartes there were two types of thinking. *Thinking based on information through the senses*, which he thought of as an <u>unreliable path to the truth</u>, and *thinking based on rational argument and objectivity*, which he believed was critical to establish knowledge. In this way he foreshadowed much of the recent work in cognitive neuroscience, as we shall see later in the book. The first type of thinking was evidence enough of one's existence, but it was the second type of thinking that got one closer to "truth."

If Descartes were around today, as well as being thrilled that France won the Soccer World Cup in 2018, he would not only friend me on Facebook but probably agree that consciousness is not the same as rationality. It can be used as proof of existence but not rationality.

This is a critical point.

The primary goal of all living organisms, including human beings *is to survive, not to enlighten the world*. We are made to adapt to our individual circumstances. That adaptation trains our brains in the behaviors, thoughts and feelings *we* need to survive in *our* particular and individual life circumstances.

In doing so we adapt, sometimes well, sometimes badly. However, our adaptive experiences shape our "beliefs" about the world.

Now this leads to a huge statement:

Beliefs are not knowledge

Our experiences lead to very specific beliefs that are a function of our individual life circumstances. *They are not generalizable to everyone.* They might be generalizable to a section of the population with certain defined characteristics. However, the best way to dig deep into the generalizability is through rational analysis, known as scientific research, which establishes "facts." And facts are quite different from beliefs, although as you shall soon see, there have been philosophers down the ages who argue that facts and beliefs are intertwined in a very complex way.

This book is therefore about Epistemology, the theory of knowledge and factors that influence its validity and scope. This should not be confused with HePissedMeOffology, which is the science of being offended. As we shall see epistemology and HePissedMeOffology (hereafter called "Offendology") are related in very complex ways.

The philosophical discussions and movements through the centuries are just as relevant today, if not more so. With knowledge exploding at a rapid pace, and everyone able to publicize their beliefs and thoughts, often as "facts", there has never been greater need for discernment and critical thinking.

In my youth there was a comedy album of Jewish humor written by Bob Booker and George Foster called "You Don't Have to be Jewish." As I recall one of the sketches went something like this.

The American and the Israeli Presidents meet. The American President comforts his Israeli counterpart about the enormity of his job by saying he is the President of 200 million people, while his counterpart governs a population of just 2 million people. The Israeli President responds.

"Mr. President, you are the President of 200 million people but I am the President of 2 million presidents."

With the enormous growth of knowledge and exposure to both facts and misinformation, many people today suddenly believe they are experts. This combined with the growing complexity brought about by an increase in knowledge, has confounded public discourse.

As we peel back the layers of very complex onions, it is easy to be misled into thinking we know all of the critical issues and how they are intertwined. For the most part, we don't, unless we have studied the field and the complexity of the key questions involved.

As complexity increases with knowledge, it becomes necessary to question underlying assumptions that have had value in the development of the concept. This has been the issue with expanding knowledge for eons. More knowledge raises more questions.

In some ways this is a book about philosophy but it isn't really about Plato, Descartes or Aristotle, it's about YOU. Your ability to see issues clearly and think critically are essential for a high quality of life. Along the way, I'll give passing reference to the historical perspective and links for those who want to know more but this book is about how to understand and better manage one of your greatest gifts, your consciousness.

It is also about US, as a community, civilization and as a race. How do we ensure that the culture of innovation and disruption brings progress rather than ultimate destruction? How do we ensure that our political systems operate for mutual benefit not just those in power? Make no mistake, the slide towards egocentrism threatens our very existence. Wherever you stand on the philosophical and political spectrum, you'd be wise to understand the factors that influence any human being's thinking.

If you think about it, there are few, if any, classes on thinking and the thought process. This book offers some suggestions to improve the thought process and it will help shine light on the ancient ideas and recent research that show how the mind works, what the problems are and how they might be overcome. I will consider what we know about how we think, and the implications of that process for us as individuals as well as a culture and a race. Along the way I will invite you to explore examples of your own thinking with questions and at the end of a book I will suggest a series of exercises that can help you be more aware of what you don't know, and how you could find out.

The purpose of this book is to show how the default setting of the mind interacts with a culture based on emotional exploitation and manipulation. Cognitive bias is as prevalent as hydrogen, so I make no apology in covering numerous ways in which distorted thinking affects many facets of our lives. My purpose is not to tell you everything I know on this subject, or everything there is to know. I make no apology for covering a lot of ground and hopefully, encouraging you to think more deeply about your thinking and explore more fully, and critically, the areas of most interest to you.

The essence of wisdom isn't having a perfect mind, it's acknowledging how imperfect the mind is.

Howard Rankin
Fall 2019

Chapter One

Is Reality an Illusion?

Reality is merely an illusion, albeit a very persistent one -- Albert Einstein

When Einstein says "Reality is merely an illusion" what does he mean?

This issue goes back centuries and has become even more relevant today. Hang in there with me for the next couple of pages because they are important and aren't just about some old dudes talking high falutin' stuff, they are relevant to topics like gender identification, gun control, gay rights, equality, your choice of cars, spouses, -- absolutely everything.

You have heard of *moral relativism*, the school of thought based on the idea that there isn't one sacred and correct standard of morals, but rather they are determined relative to a particular culture or environment. Thus, no particular morality or moral principle is "right" – it just depends on various prevailing circumstances. As a result, what might be seen as a sin in one culture, might be completely acceptable in another. According to this philosophy, there's no overarching, fundamental true morality, it is all constructed.

Similarly, there is *cognitive relativism* which also argues that there isn't an overarching "truth" but that it, too, is constructed and relative to a variety of factors, like culture and even human understanding.

Protagoras, a famous philosopher who lived about 2500 years ago, asserted that "man is the measure of all things -- of things that are, that they are, and of things that are not, that they are not." In other words, truth and knowledge are a function of human beings and human variables and don't reflect any independent and objective reality.

Plato objected that this relativism eliminates the distinction between truth and falsehood; if each individual is really the "measure of what is" then each person would be infallible.

An excellent article by Emrys Westacott, summarizes these debates about knowledge and reality. Professor Westacott is the author of many works including *The Wisdom of Frugality: Why Less Is More - More or Less.*

(This was from an article on Cognitive Relativism that appeared in the Internet Encyclopedia of Philosophy https://www.iep.utm.edu/cog-rel/)

Westacott writes:

"Plato argued that if Protagoras is right, then whatever a person thinks is true, is true. But in that case, Protagoras must concede that those who think relativism is false are correct. So, if Protagorean relativism is true, it must also be false."

That Plato was one smart guy.

The philosopher Immanuel Kant also chimed in on the debate.

According to Westacott, Kant's position was that…

"The judgments we call true are true for us and of our world; but to claim they are true in the sense of describing an independently existing reality is to go beyond what we can meaningfully or justifiably assert."

"Kant is not generally considered a relativist since he held that the forms our mind imposes on the world are common to all human beings. Truths like the truths of geometry or the statement that every event is caused are thus universally accepted and constitute a priori knowledge. The forms we impose on experience also give the world a certain necessary character that is independent of our beliefs and wishes. For instance, causes must precede their effect, and time can only flow in one direction.[1] In this sense, the forms confer objectivity on the world we experience, and our well-founded judgments about that world can be called objectively true. Later thinkers, however, took Kant's ideas further down the road toward fully-fledged relativism. Hegel, while upholding a concept of "absolute knowledge", allows every stage that human consciousness has passed through in the historical development of civilization to express an outlook that is true in a partial way."

Now let's take the logical leap from Kant and Hegel to ads about weight loss.

Maybe you have seen a commercial for a weight loss product in which three people, ideally celebrities, all say, "This is the best weight loss program ever!" That is a belief not a fact. For it to have some factual accuracy, the program would have to be reliably compared to all other weight loss programs, using hundreds of thousands of subjects over a fairly long time. Until then we would have to say, "Results not typical" (i.e. not factual) which would be a good mantra for our own thoughts and beliefs: Results (Beliefs) not typical (or generalizable).

---

[1] Although there is some interesting quantum research that suggests that causes can actually precede effects. One of my favorite stories on this topic is about a series of papers on this very subject written by physicist Richard Feynman. Because of an administrative error, Part 2 of the series on effects preceding causes was actually printed before Part 1!

However, there are relativists who decry objective knowledge and this has led to the over emphasis on subjective experience.

Westacott provides these quotes from various famous philosophers.

"Reason is whatever the norms of the local culture believe it to be".[2]

"The choice between competing theories is arbitrary, since there is no such thing as objective truth."[3]

"There is no unique truth, no unique objective reality." [4]

"There is nothing to be said about either truth or rationality apart from descriptions of the familiar procedures of justification which a given society—ours—uses in one area of enquiry,"[5]

The issue of cognitive relativism is very relevant in the discussion of cognitive bias and fake news.

When people effectively state that "this is my reality," that is one thing, but then when they use that to presume they are right and you are wrong, they are being completely illogical if not hypocritical. Indeed the first rule of Offendology is that...

---

[2] (Hilary Putnam, Realism and Reason: Philosophical Papers, Volume 3 (Cambridge, 1983), p. 235.)

[3] Karl Popper, The Open Society and its Enemies, Vol. II (London, 1963), p. 369f.)

[4] (Ernest Gellner, Relativism and the Social Sciences (Cambridge, 1985), p. 84.)

[5]Richard Rorty, Objectivity, Relativism and Truth: Philosophical Papers, Volume 1 (Cambridge, 1991), p. 23.)

If you indeed take the relativist position of knowledge and truth, then you have to accept that anyone's view is legitimate because relativism is based in the fact that there is no overarching truth.

You thus can't *vehemently claim* that your view is superior because it entails the proposition that everyone's truth is equally justified.

And fostering the idea that truth is personal can lead to the dissemination of several destructive ideas in the clash between personal reality and objective truth.

Rankin, Rankin & Rankin Attorneys at Law*
Class Action Suit vs. Gravity
If you are a man over 196 pounds or a woman over 156 pounds you have been discriminated against by gravity. As a result we are filing a class action as well as a Supreme Court Petition to have Gravity ruled discriminatory and unconstitutional. Because Gravity unfairly exerts extra force on those who, for one reason or another, are bigger than the mean in weight for their gender, this represents a discriminatory bias and you might be entitled to compensation.

*Disclaimer: This is merely an illustration, also what used to be known as 'a joke.' The people mentioned in this piece are merely fictional and any resemblance to real people is entirely unintended and coincidental. As far as I know, at the time of writing, there is no legal action being sought against gravity and no one is likely to gain any compensation therefrom. The paragraph is just illustrative of what can happen when applying social constructions, like political correctness, to forces in the physical world. No animals were harmed in writing this paragraph.

One of the issues with moral and cognitive relativists today is that they fail to see the hypocrisy and illogicality of *being strident* about relativistic views. As a result, they often come across as pompous hypocrites which does their causes no favors. Yes, of course, there are often many perspectives to an issue, many of which are legitimate. And human biases do indeed creep into the understanding and creation of knowledge. However, that is only a valuable perspective if there is then a logical dialog about them, not a shouting match about which one is "right" based on emotions.

You can also take the position that while there are indeed contributing human factors to truth and knowledge, like culture and language, there is also a very practical value in agreeing on proven principles that work within a given framework, without necessarily elevating them to universal, inviolable principles. Indeed, any of the ideas expressed in the rest of the book, have been passed down through the centuries by many sages of different cultures.

For example, the concept of gravity had been refined and evolved over the centuries but it is a useful concept and knowledge of it has led Man to be able to make some amazing technological advances.

Recognizing that knowledge constantly changes doesn't render it useless or illegitimate.

Given the above discussion about knowledge and the influence of human and personal factors, it is important to understand what those factors are and how they operate. That is the point of this book.

The difference between genius and stupidity is that genius has its limits. -- Einstein

Chapter Two

Logic

I believe that some of the problem with thinking is that many of us don't understand the simple principles of logic. These are important, but easily explainable. At the end of the book there is a recommendation for online courses, some of which are free, in critical thinking and logic if you want to pursue this more. [6]

Here are the logic basics.

A logical argument consists of a premise, evidence and a conclusion.

Premise: All broccoli is green
Evidence: This vegetable is broccoli
Conclusion: This vegetable is green

Now, because of a variety of factors that I will explain during the remainder of this book, it's very easy to make logical errors.

Premise: All broccoli is green
Evidence: This vegetable is green
Conclusion: This vegetable is broccoli.

It's very easy to confuse aspects of the premise so that you take a necessary condition of a subject, the greenness of broccoli, and generalize it to all green things rather than generalizing it just to the broccoli.

Another issue is that we take our individual experience and beliefs and use them as evidence, for or against, a premise.

---

[6] Isn't online education today amazing!? I just got my brain surgeon certification for just $25!

For example:

"This has been the coolest summer I can remember, which proves there's no such thing as global warming."

This is a misunderstanding about the premise "global warming", which is that the temperature on the planet Earth shows a rising trend. Global warming really says nothing about an individual or several locations on the planet, neither does it rule out that some places might actually be cooling.

"This is the warmest summer I can remember, which proves global warming.

No, it doesn't, because of the conditions associated with the concept of "global warming" described above.

Remember: Results (Beliefs) not typical, (or generalizable.)

These are great examples of how we as individuals use our own experiences to explain concepts and "facts" that can't be explained or proven by individual experience.

Oh, Descartes just sent me a "like."

Self-Limiting Beliefs
The concept of self-limiting beliefs is a very popular notion among coaches and health professionals. There must be at least three trillion books about the subject. However, the popular notion of self-limiting beliefs, is in itself limiting.

Yes, of course, we are exposed to cultural, parental, marketing and other sources of messages either directly about us, or that by implication describe us. Indeed, we need to recognize and see the flaws (and sometimes the truth in them). However, much of the impact, even damage, of self-limiting beliefs comes from faulty reasoning, either implicit in the message itself or by how you (re) construct it.

Premise: All smart people have a college degree
Evidence: I don't have a college degree
Conclusion: Therefore I am not smart.

Can you see the error in that thinking?

The premise is inaccurate. Not all smart people have a college degree.

How about this one?

Premise: If you have a college degree, you are smart
Evidence: I don't have a college degree
Conclusion: Therefore I am not smart

The conclusion is false, because the premise allows even people who don't have a college degree to be smart.

Premise: I always screw up
Evidence: I am doing a project
Conclusion: I will screw this project up.

The conclusion is logical but the premise is clearly an exaggeration for the vast majority of people.

It is helpful to write your beliefs, self-limiting or otherwise, down in the format of Premise, Evidence, Conclusion.

Examine the premise. Is it true?
Examine the evidence. Where does the evidence come from? How accurate is it? Is it described in all-or-nothing terms?
Examine the Conclusion. Is it logical?

Now, if it were that simple, life would be a whole lot easier. However, there are certain aspects of human consciousness that complicate matters. These include the limitation of language, the nature of perception and memory, the problem of relativity and binary thinking, the nature of "facts", cognitive biases, defense mechanisms, and the role of emotion in the thought (or lack of thought) process, as well as external influences, like culture and environment. This book examines all of these factors and how they impact your thinking process.

First, however, a quick look at "thinking."

Chapter Three

What is Thinking?

A thorough research of the psychological literature (don't sweat, I've done it for you), will show that there has been a recent surge of interest in how the mind works, largely led by the work of Daniel Kahneman and others. Kahneman's book *Thinking, Fast and Slow* is a wonderful analysis of decades of cognitive research and succinctly explains how human beings are mostly intuitive rather than rational. 'Intuitive' here means tapping into the vague subconscious that contains untold associations and memories that evade focused attention and shape our perception and narratives.

Perception is reality but it is *our* reality not *the* reality. We need to feel in control and to do so we create narratives designed to do just that -- make us believe we have control. The reality, however, is different. For the most part, we don't have control, just the illusion of it, but that's still better than acknowledging the alternative.

What is Thinking?
If you think about it, thinking can refer to several different processes. In one way, anything that comes into your mind, either from immediate sensory processing or after considered analysis, is thinking. There are several processes, I think.

External Sensory Processing. This is mostly an automatic and unconscious process. For example, you hear something and quickly interpret the noise, unconsciously analyzing many aspects of the input; loudness, direction, timbre, etc. You then make a judgment about what the noise is and where it is coming from. A lot of thinking is like this and we take it for granted. Indeed, we do not subject the vast majority of these sensory impressions and our interpretation thereof, to any critical or real, conscious analysis. This would be way too time consuming and unproductive most of the time and the brain is interested in conserving energy for more important issues.

Internal processing. This is an analysis of your internal state, be that thought or a physical feeling. You experience a physical sensation or have a thought and quickly create a narrative about it, often involving judgment. Or you have a thought and simply accept it. This is often an unconscious process. While you're aware of the outcome -- the story in your head -- you're not aware of the process.

Consciously analyzing these internal narratives is a skill that is underutilized. We're too busy to spend time thinking about our thinking. Moreover, this same process applies to the assessment of our emotions. We subconsciously analyze our feelings and decide what they are. As we shall see, thought and emotions aren't as separate as we like to think.

Rational analysis. This is what Kahneman calls *System 2 thinking*. It requires an understanding of logic and statistics, is hard work and actually activates the stress response. This requires stepping back from the automatic response to external or internal impressions and trying to logically analyze rather than just accept your first instinctive reaction. This analysis is done using a different part of your brain, the frontal lobe, and is less influenced by the emotional/survival areas of the brain. In this way, Kahneman is reflecting Descartes' views: that there is sensory input, adaptation and beliefs, and then there is critical thinking and rationality.

> *Few people think more than two or three times a year; I have made an international reputation for myself by thinking once or twice a week. - George Bernard Shaw*

On the face of it Shaw's quote seems like one of his typical sarcastic swipes at humanity but on closer analysis perhaps it tells us a lot about the lack of close analysis. It depends what the term "think" means. But if it means Kahneman's System 2 thinking, an open-minded deep dive into a subject to examine it without judgment, then perhaps the quote is accurate. Perhaps many people don't do that more than a few times a year, if at all.

Experiencing rather than processing. The problem with processing as described above is that we get consumed with the object of our processing. For example, when you focus on either an object or even a thought, it becomes the center of attention and drives your emotional response and even more thoughts. In short, you are mentally *reacting* to the stimulus. In his excellent bestseller *The Untethered Soul*, author Michael Singer makes the point that people assume they are defined by this chatter and response but in fact what really defines us is the ability to be conscious of our consciousness. This involves techniques like mindfulness and meditation where you are *neither interpreting nor analyzing but experiencing*. The idea is to develop experiencing without judgment. This, too, requires a lot of effort and practice.

In addition, our thought processes are influenced by our past experiences and pre-dispositions. The brain is limited in that we can't possibly remember all of these influential factors so they remain hidden from view, influencing our thought process, what the American psychologist William James called "the fringe of consciousness."

These are complex processes and it's hardly surprising that the energy-conserving brain has found some simple shortcuts to make life easier. Indeed, energy consumption is critical. The brain needs to conserve energy for times of threat. The two-pound blob at the top of your neck actually uses 25% of your body's energy so we try not to use it unless we have to. Imagine you had a car that did five miles to the gallon. You'd only use it when absolutely necessary, the rest of the time you would use your hybrid vehicle that gets ten times the mileage. Under serious threat, the autonomic nervous system takes over and it has a role in what the famous Stanford psychiatrist Karl Pribram called the four Fs: "Fight, flight, fear and sex."

Because of the importance of the flight/fight response it has prominence in almost every area of our thinking process: perception, attention, and memory. We are made to be more sensitive to threat, and thus overvalue fear, which impacts every aspect of our lives. Threat is the primary lens through which we look at life. Not surprisingly perhaps, a study at Penn State[7] suggested that there are more negative words in a language than positive ones. Threat is more important than happiness or pleasure, at least to the brain, the guardian of our survival, which is constantly vigilant. The brain never goes to sleep although it sends us into sleep so it can do some important work like filing away memories and clearing the brain of toxic material.

As a result, we have an inbuilt need to feel we have control, which requires 'knowledge' of what's going on. Those two needs drive us to be story-tellers not truth-seekers. And, as you'll see, our thoughts and emotions are connected in a surprising way.

Our interaction with both our internal and external environments, is a function of several key factors. Perception is complex.

Piaget's Stages of Cognitive Development
Piaget was a Swiss psychologist who is best known for his description of the four stages of cognitive development. He argued that children weren't less intelligent than adults, rather they had yet to develop different levels of cognition and mental operations. Of course, he was right, there are many children -- even very young children -- who are smarter than many adults. And interestingly

---

[7] (Schrauf, Robert W. and Julia Sanchez (2004). The preponderance of negative emotion words across generations and across cultures. Journal of Multilingual and Multicultural Development, 25(2-3), 266-284.)

there is some new neuro-linguistic research that suggests that young children haven't yet developed the binary brain.

Despite the fact that there is criticism of Piaget's four stages, it is still a useful guide to cognitive development. However, he missed out an important fifth stage.

Here are his stages of cognitive development.

1. The Sensori-Motor stage. Learning is through sensory experience and the manipulation of objects.

2. The Pre-Operational stage. Learning is through pretend play but logic and understanding other's perspectives is elusive

3. The Concrete Operational stage. In this stage children can understand logic but tend to be rigid in their thinking.

4. The Formal Operational Stage. This stage involves an increase in logic and the ability to think abstractly.

Now it's one thing to understand logic and abstract ideas but it's another to use them. My proposed fifth stage is about understanding the thought process, the story-telling nature of the brain and the difference between logic and rationalization, especially in relation to our own thinking. I propose to call this...

The Operational Insight Stage. Here there is true insight into whether you are engaging in thoughtful, rational thinking, or just telling yourself -- and others -- narratives and are really just in Building Stories (BS) mode.

The thought process depends heavily on the perception of events, which presents another set of problems.

Questions

1. Has anyone ever taught you about the thought process?
2. Do you think that teaching students about the thinking process would be helpful?
3. Do you ever challenge your beliefs, or merely defend them?

Chapter Four

The Problem of Perception

A gunshot rings out.

Bill hears it and assumes someone is hunting. Immediately, his mind is full of images of all the fun times he has had hunting with his friends. An automatic smile conquers his face, and as those memories flood his consciousness, he is filled with neuro-chemicals that relax him and put him in an almost euphoric mood. He feels the gratitude for his good friends and the many great times they have had together.

Joe hears the gunshot, too. His body immediately tenses up and the fight/flight system goes into gear pumping out stress chemicals like adrenaline and cortisol. A darkness descends on him as he struggles to NOT think about that fateful day in Afghanistan when he and his platoon were caught in the crossfire of a vicious gunfight. Tears start streaming down his face, as he fails to repress the images of his buddies, lying dead in pools of blood in a foreign land.

Oh, and it wasn't even a gunshot. It was the loud backfiring of an engine.

That our perceptions are significantly influenced by our past experiences and memories, is undeniable. The cause of one man's delighted laughter is the source of another man's soul-destroying sadness. Previous experiences have trained our brain to react to cues, especially if they have strong emotional associations, which have been learned naturally by experience. They create an architecture that shapes our reality. But it's OUR reality, not a universal reality. And if it's not universal, can it be a "reality"?

The problem is that most of the time we don't know about other people's conscious narratives and subconscious cues – and neither do we make an effort to find out, unless we're in the business of counseling or psychotherapy. As a result, we have no idea how to walk in their shoes. In fact, our views about people are often based on one or two "facts" that might not even be true and might even have been manipulated to influence us. Moreover, many of us don't even know how to walk in our own shoes. We are overcome by emotional states that direct our thinking and sabotage us in many ways. (I'm working on another book as you read this: *The Art of Walking in Shoes.*)

One of the reasons that all the wise men of the past stress the need for compassion, is the realization that we all come from different experiences and unless you understand those experiences you can't judge or even emotionally react to another. Remember the key point about our "thinking"; Results (experiences) not typical.

However, past experience and associations are not the only variables that influence our perceptions.

The Power of Context
Context is a big determinant of how we react and perceive sensory impressions. For example, if Joe were sitting in or near the pits of a NASCAR race, he would interpret the noise as backfiring exhaust and it would probably not create anything like the response when he was "surprised" by the "gunshot" in the above example. Sure, he might at first have an emotional response but if he were sitting there long enough and heard constant backfiring, he would likely not have the same level of response as in the earlier example and after time, he might not have a response at all.

Our constructed context is a big determinant of how we actually perceive events. You would perceive someone walking down the street dressed as Napoleon quite differently if you saw the exact same scene after having left a costume party, the theme of which was historical French figures, than if you had no such pre-perception experience.

It turns out that context is critical in thinking and in wisdom. Human beings *might* be the only species on the earth that have the ability to understand and take contexts other than their own into account, but we rarely do. The plea to walk in someone else's shoes, is a plea to understand other people's, and other creatures, contexts. Without that, you can't really understand their behavior. Now understanding doesn't necessarily imply acceptance or tolerance but we'll get to that later.

Defining the context and adapting it accordingly might just be the key to not just success, but meaning, too. Viktor Frankl's successful search for meaning in the hell of a concentration camp speaks eloquently to the role context has in the perception and pursuit of purpose in any circumstance.

I believe that life, all life from lowest animals to human beings, is about encountering new contexts and adapting to them successfully. Where there's no adaptation, there won't be survival or happiness. So, the perception of context, whether consciously appreciated or not, is critical for all living creatures. And we have to understand the benefits but also the limitations from looking at life through the human lens.

Let's consider human beings' views of animals. The prevailing view in science has been that we shouldn't imbue animals with human characteristics. This is called *anthropomorphism* – literally, the attribution of human characteristics to non-human beings. However, this concept is egotistical as well as erroneous, in that it assumes that just because humans have certain abilities these must, therefore, only be human. And, by the way, just because humans have the *capacity* to perform certain cognitive tasks, for example, doesn't mean that they do. We need to be careful in applying anthropomorphism to humans as well as animals.

The rise of science and rationality has also misled human beings. In fact, almost any activity will mislead, because it's human. That doesn't mean we should abandon rational enquiry – far from it – but like everything else it has been misunderstood.

Consider the Russian physiologist Pavlov's famous work on conditioning dogs to perform behaviors by 'reinforcing' them with food. The human takeaway from this work is that dogs can be 'conditioned' by giving them food. The canine takeaway from this experiment is that Russian scientists can be conditioned to give dogs food. The emphasis on pure rationality and objectivity can be misleading because activity is conducted by humans and more importantly, the *results interpreted by humans*.

More recently, there has been greater realization that if you try to understand the animal's context, you will find a much richer array of skills than if you expect them to perform in the human context.

Frans De Waal is one of my favorite writers. An experienced primatologist who writes superbly, he sheds enormous insights into the world of animals, and thus human beings. From his *Our Inner Ape* to the more recent *Are We Smart Enough to Know How Smart Animals Are?* the bestselling author shows how failing to understand the animal context has led to false data and beliefs about animal skills and especially cognition.

He cites several examples in *Are We Smart Enough to Know How Smart Animals Are?*

De Waal writes about one famous study, conducted by Edward Thorndike in 1898 with cats that led to the *Thorndike Effect*.

In this study, cats' behavior was shaped by food rewards, so that they rubbed the side of the cage with their heads, thus opening the door of the cage. This experiment was heralded at the time as showing that even seemingly adaptive intelligent behavior could be conditioned.

However, when Susan Stuttard and Bruce Moore repeated the experiment with friendly welcomes and no food, the cats performed the exact same behavior without "reward" because cats naturally rub their head or flank against the object of their affection or nearby objects. This was their natural behavior. This wasn't a case of conditioning at all,… well, not of the cats. The researcher's belief was conditioned because they had failed to look outside their own cognitive cages. And a lot of perfectly good cat food was wasted in the process.

And here's a blog I once drafted for an addiction treatment outfit.

On Rats and Addiction

In his book <u>Our Inner Ape</u>, renowned primatologist Frans DeWaal, points out that the humble and much maligned rat has some social intelligence. "To compare a politician to a rat is unfair – to the rat," he writes. The under-rated rat has featured in many addiction studies and has something to say about addiction.

In fact, there's been millions of dollars spent on animal research in addiction. Most of it has been done with laboratory rats and mice. Such studies have looked at the genetics of alcohol metabolism, others at the conditions under which these small creatures can develop dependence, and yet others on withdrawal. One of my favorite studies showed that if heroin dependent rats were withdrawn in novel cages rather than the cages in which they were addicted, the withdrawal symptoms were much less severe. In other words, environmental cues effect drug use and withdrawal.

Recently, however, my faith in some of this research was severely shaken. It's a long story but it has to do with my mother's cousin, who actually conducted some of this research in the 1970s. He recently died and his family had to sort through his possessions. In doing so, amongst some very old papers, they made an amazing discovery. It's so astounding that I will simply let it speak for itself. This was found on a very tattered piece of parchment paper.

"My name is Arnold and I'm a rat. I was actually number C1143326 in my laboratory and I participated in a number of alcohol studies. I have written this in the hope that after my death the real truth about addiction among rats – and humans -- will be revealed.

"You people are stupid! In my first experiment, I was given access to alcohol and I drank it – as much as I could get. Honestly, I didn't like the taste at all or how it made me feel but when you're locked up in a very small cage, isolated from your fellow rats, with absolutely nothing to do, take it from me, you will DRINK ANYTHING! You will DO ANYTHING because life in solitary confinement with no stimulation is SO BORING and SOUL DESTROYING. Would prisoners in solitary confinement with no stimulation drink a gin and tonic if they found it in their cells?? Of course, they would. Would their actions tell us about addiction or solitary confinement?

"And that withdrawal experiment, where rats did better coming off heroin in novel cages rather than the ones associated with heroin ingestion, needs to be "interpreted with caution," as my fellow handlers used to say. I knew several rats in that experiment and they told me that when they were moved to the novel cages it was like going from the Comfort Inn to the Ritz! The novel cages were so much nicer, airier, not so smelly, it was like going on vacation. That's why they did better.

"Being a laboratory rat is no fun. It's like being in perpetual solitary confinement. It's miserable. I started a book when I was suffering in my cage called Rat's Search For Meaning. I think that we rats, like you humans, need social connection, stimulation,

*purpose, and when those are taken away you don't give a rat's...
well, you just don't care about anything. You're disconnected.
That's when you want to drink or snort cocaine. It's not really the
physical cage you're in, it's the psychological and spiritual one
that makes you want to use."*

"So, as much as you people think you are – you're not rat-ional."

*Arnold, despite his small furry body, whiskers and less than stellar
reputation, has a point.*

As De Waal states ...

"The lesson is before scientists test any animal, they need to know
its typical behavior. The power of conditioning is not in doubt, but
the early investigators had totally overlooked a critical piece of
information. They had not, as recommended by Lorenz, considered
the whole organism. Animals show many unconditional responses,
or behavior that develops naturally in all members of the species.
Reward and punishment may affect such behavior but cannot take
credit creating it." (p.21)

When my wife and I get ready for church, our dog Jack takes up a
position on his bed and gets ready for sleep.

"Jack, knows it's Sunday and we're going to church," I say to my
wife.

"Don't be an anthropomorphic idiot," I can hear you say, "Dogs
don't know the days of the week or anything about church!"

But then Jack says, "Well, I know the smell of those clothes and
when he wears them he's generally gone for a couple of hours."

There's more about science and pseudoscience later in the book.
For now it's critical to appreciate that context is the key to

understanding the behavior of any species – especially the human species. That's why it is often better to know the right questions rather than the answers.

I have explored many of the cognitive biases but I have yet come across one that has formally labeled *the tendency to overestimate human capacities and under-estimate animal capabilities*. I propose to call this the **DeWaal Effect**, in honor of Dr. Frans' amazing work in this field.

Another big factor in perception is the presence of already existing narratives.

For example, if you see someone you dislike intensely apparently helping an old lady across the street, are you likely to think, "That's a nice gesture" or "That bastard is probably going to rob her blind"?

We have a need for coherence in our narratives and beliefs; change is hard and energy consuming. To have a positive perception of something or someone who was to this point perceived negatively, we have to rearrange our narratives, which we don't really want to do. Thus, we will come up with all sorts of reasons and thoughts to reconcile new and previous narratives.

In the above example, we might justify his apparently thoughtful behavior as follows:

- I bet that's his mom
- Perhaps he is high on pot
- Maybe he has gone to rehab
- Is that really him or someone that looks like him?

These and similar thoughts are much more likely than a reorganization of your previous narratives such as…

- Perhaps I have misjudged him all these years.

Note, too, that if you saw your best friend *doing the exact same thing*, seemingly walking an old lady across the road, you might tear up at the sight and spawn the oxytocin-induced narrative, "That's why I love her so much. She's so awesome!"

Human beings want control and consistency, which is why changing anything, except our clothes but especially our minds, is difficult and not the first option.

And another factor in perception is your cognitive state. If you were feeling in a great mood because you just won a few hundred bucks on the lottery, you are probably more likely to cut the guy you dislike in the above example some slack, than if you were having a really bad day.

There is some classic research on this, which suggests physical as well as cognitive states are critical in perception. One study showed judges were more likely to hand out more severe sentences or deny parole the hungrier they got.[8]

Another big problem is that the human mind has a limited capacity. We can't remember every relevant memory that pertains to any situation. If we work at it, we might be conscious of a few relevant instances; the remainder lurk in our subconscious, casting an influential but murky shadow, what the nineteenth century psychologist William James called "the fringe of consciousness" that was mentioned earlier. While consciously we are registering the sensory impression of what lies in front of us, the hidden emotions and memories of the fringe of consciousness shape our perceptions, assumptions, judgments and narratives of what we think we see, hear, feel, smell and taste.

---

[8] Shai Danziger et al., Extraneous Factors in Judicial Decisions, 108Proc., Natl Acad. Sci. 17, 6889-92 (2011).

The key to our perceptions and narratives is emotion. Emotion is the fuel on which our mental vehicle runs. Emotion influences memory, which is important to cognitive bias. For example, *the availability bias* is a function of how many relevant instances we can recall about a topic. The more we can recall, the more we value the content of those memories. It doesn't matter whether those memories are accurate or not, they are the "data" on which we base our narratives. This is why media coverage – and social media -- is so critical in shaping views and opinions -- it provides the "data" on which we base our beliefs and thought processes. That's also the case with pseudoscience where spurious and questionable beliefs are touted as facts borne out by rational enquiry. Memory is, of course, notoriously unreliable and can easily be hijacked by emotion. Indeed, a lot of the time it's the accompanying emotion that will determine how a memory is encoded and recalled.

Because of the dominant role of emotion, we live in the present. You might imagine how you will feel in the future, but it is the emotion in the NOW that is so critical. As a result, we overvalue the present and tend to discount the future, a phenomenon known as *temporal discounting*. Which, for example, is why a majority of people don't save effectively for their retirement.

However, even when we are not dealing with thought processes that are fueled by strong emotions, errors creep in often making our perceptions and memories unreliable.

Perception is Illusion
Our perceptions are also a function of contrast, the brain's need for simplicity and speed, our emotions and our environment, to name just a few variables. A good example of this concept can be found in the book *Sleights of Mind* written by neuroscientists Stephen Macknik, and Susana Martinez-Conde who studied illusion and magic. What they discovered is all of those magic tricks simply

take advantage of the brain's need for speed, simplicity and contrast, to manipulate cognitive bias and thus perception. For example, if you show someone four playing cards very quickly and three of them are black, the brain will automatically look at the red card first. Withdraw the cards before there's time to examine them further, and there's a high percentage chance that the card that will be remembered is the red card. Hey presto! Abracadabra! You're an illusionist.

Illusion, however, is much more common than just in magic shows.

Perception is, therefore, *an individualized reconstruction* and not a perfect representation of reality. It is a construction created by our personal experiences, biases, context and environment. We are illusionists. The brain is so malleable that it caters to our personal circumstances and doesn't provide a standardized output. Moreover…

As amazing as the brain is, it is still a very limited organ

There are many animals whose brains have much more power than the human brain in one respect or another. For example, dogs have a sense of smell that is about 60 times better than humans. Dolphins and other animals have the power of echolocation. The fact is that the human brain is limited and can therefore, only "know" so much. *We need to understand we view the world through a very particular and limited lens, totally colored by personal experience and human skills and limitations as well as contextual variables.*

This all sounds very arbitrary. How can that be when we often feel so very sure of our thoughts and perceptions? Well, those thoughts and perceptions are created because they make so much sense to us, even if they're "wrong" or not shared by others.

In addition, humans overvalue their potential because we have managed to "control" the other species on the planet, which significantly over-inflates our sense of our capabilities. For Heaven's sakes we can barely make it to the nearest planets in our solar system, let alone other solar systems, let alone other galaxies. Just because we can get one over on a panda or a kangaroo doesn't make us kings of the galaxy.

A typical response to the notion that we have a limited and biased brain might be:

"Yes, well that's great, Doc, but it's the only brain we have got, so get over it."

Even if that were 100% true, that response is still a classic deflection and does nothing to address the limited nature of the brain. In addition, **reflection rather than deflection** might question whether it really is the "only brain we have." In other words, is it possible to retrain our brains to achieve more complex processing than we currently think possible?

There is some current work using AI which attempts to do this. For example, Elon Musk's Neuralink is exploring human brain to computer interfaces. Bryan Johnson's Kernel is similarly trying to "radically improve and expand human cognition." (see more at www.kernel.co)

It is surely convenient to accept our customized perceptions and memories and we often make no attempt to look beyond them. However, that doesn't mean our brains are not capable of doing just that. The fact that we settle for a convenient and comfortable cognitive functioning doesn't mean that the brain isn't capable of far more.

The Problem of Memory

We've known for some time that memory is not a reliable recorder of our experience but is instead very vulnerable to bias and distortion at every stage of the process, from the immediate encoding of our sense experiences (see above comments about perception) to recall at any particular time. Given that our sensory input is distorted, the initial memory is an individualized and subjective snapshot of experience. Then many factors, from emotion to other people, influence the recall of the event at any one time.

Each time we remember something, we recreate the memory and it is subject to distortion by factors present at the time of the recall as well as events that have occurred in the intervening time since the original experience. Elizabeth Loftus' research shows that we have a *misinformation effect*, that memory can be hijacked, by accident or design, by what others say about it. For example, in her research, the recall of a photo of a car accident was significantly influenced by whether people were told the cars *hit* each other or *smashed* into each other. When subjects were told of the cars smashing into each other they recalled broken glass in the photo when there was none. In a Stanford University experiment, whether crime in an area was described as a "wild beast" or a "virus" influenced the remedies subjects suggested for it.

Loftus also showed that childhood memories could be implanted, with 25% of subjects buying into the suggested idea that they had been lost in a mall as a child. This and other research led to bitter disagreements as therapists, who used regressive and hypnotic techniques, defended themselves against accusations that they were planting false memories. Loftus herself talks about the "fiction of memory." However, what we are witnessing is the binary brain once again rising is two-sided head. While Loftus and others have shown that memories *can* be implanted, it doesn't mean that all memory is a fiction and that all memories are false. Memory is a reconstruction and subject to bias and distortion, which *can* lead to inaccuracies.

Cognitive distortion therefore is a product of emotion and memory. I can express this as follows, where C^2 is cognitive distortion, E is emotion, and M is memory. Memory here is measured by strength not accuracy. Emotion is the strength of emotion; powerful emotions could include, for example, extreme stress, deep depression or romantic love. So the formula is:

$C^2=EM$ (or something like that.)

This is disconcertingly similar to another famous equation, Einstein's Theory of Relativity.

As mentioned above, it turns out relativity is a major problem for human beings.

Similar to Einstein's theory of Relativity, **Rankin's Theory of Relatives** states that when family members come to stay, space shortens and time lengthens.

The **Theory of Cognitive Relativity** highlights the fact that it is very difficult for our minds to attribute relative weights to different ideas and concepts. This is a problem because human beings can only focus on one thing at a time. Multi-tasking is really task-switching; we can focus on something for a short time, then switch and hopefully we can switch back again before we have lost too much of our focus. But when you are focusing on a concept it has your entire attention and emotional response. For those few seconds, or even less, everything else is blocked out. If you want to compare A, B, and C, you have to drop A to focus on B, then drop B to focus on C. *You can't experience them all at once.*

This is something like a **Cognitive Uncertainty Principle** in that as soon as you try to shine a light on an idea, it changes because of the focus and the initial perception. Moreover, the context and the words used, the lens through which the idea is viewed, influence the perception.

Nothing in life is quite as important as you think it is while you're thinking about it. – Daniel Kahneman

In addition, we are constantly misled by our focus and initial perspective. Kahneman gives a great example of this in *Thinking, Fast and Slow.*

"The *lowest* rates of kidney cancer occur in small, rural communities."

When you hear or read this statement you are likely to start creating an explanation, a narrative, about this fact. One could easily imagine coming up with all sorts of ideas for why the rates of kidney cancer would be lower in small, rural communities. Stress, lifestyle, nutrition are factors that might be invoked to explain this fact.

Here's the next piece of information.

"The *highest* rate of kidney cancer occurs in small, rural communities."

What's going on? Kahneman's tricking us! No, he isn't. The conundrum is a function *of sampling bias.* In a small community there will often be no cases of kidney cancer resulting in the lowest rates. However, if there are one or two cases, the rate in small community will be disproportionately high. It's the small sample that is the issue here and it has nothing to do with kidney cancer. However, if you have never been exposed to statistics, the sample size issue might easily elude you. Moreover, your initial perception will anchor your thinking, making it difficult to accommodate new perception.

As a result of these biases, assigning relative weight is very demanding and difficult if not impossible. It's a whole lot easier to go with the binary brain and turn the issue into a choice between over-simplified alternatives. This is especially true when we recognize that emotion is an important driver of consciousness. Emotions tend to be all-or-nothing. Yes, we might say "we're a little pissed off" but it is really difficult to distinguish gradations of emotion. We're either angry or we're not, frustrated or we're not. When was the last time you heard anyone say, "I'm about 63% frustrated right now"?

Higher levels of consciousness all the way up to an "all-knowing God" are assumed to be able to know the entire universe of possibilities and ideally experience them all at once to be able to make relative judgments. This Higher Power enables a balanced, relative view devoid of personal biases and emotion. Unfortunately, most of us are stuck with a much Lower Power (see chapter 12). One of the problems of assigning relative weights to different aspects of a concept or perception is language. Words can be a real problem.

"We are what we think. All that we are arises with our thoughts. With our thoughts, we make the world." -- Buddha

Questions
1. Do you always assume that your memory is 100% accurate?
2. Do you recognize the role of emotions in your thoughts and ideas?
3. Are you aware of the critical experiences that shape your perceptions and narratives?
4. What are they?

Chapter Five

Words, Language and the Deep Dive

With the development of language, Man was given a new tool with which to describe the world. Great, now Man could accurately describe what was happening in the world and communicate effectively. Well, not quite. It turns out that words don't just *describe* our perception, *they actually influence it*. Because this is a book and contains words, it is important to understand the role of words in shaping our experiences, including your perception of what you read in this, or any other book, or anywhere else.

Words are like silos. They divide the world. They are the restricted lens through which we describe our experience. Words convey certain characteristics, which means they also create *distinctions*.

Words are processed in different areas of the brain depending on their meaning. The same word, for example "passed," is processed in different areas of the brain depending on the meaning. There is a difference in where these three versions of the word "passed" are processed.

- His mother passed last week after a long battle with cancer.

- The quarterback passed on fourth and one

- We passed the palace on our way back from our trip

Words have multiple meanings and most are simple descriptions that try to categorize the world. A lot of the work in this *area* (multiple meaning word) has been *conducted* (multiple meaning word) by researchers who have looked at where words are *processed* (multiple meaning word) in the *structure* (multiple meaning word) of the *brain* (multiple meaning word).

It is thought that the meanings of words and language are represented in a semantic system distributed across much of the cerebral cortex. Alex Huth, Jack Gallant and their colleagues have started to map where different meanings are processed in brain. For example, the right prefrontal cortex is associated with words that connote places, times and numbers. These findings seem to be consistent across subjects but will clearly be more refined by future research.

For more information please visit http://gallantlab.org/huth2016/

Given the precedence of the fight/flight autonomic nervous system it should be no surprise that emotionally charged words are especially salient, attract more attention, are more quickly processed and connect with the structures in the brain responsible for emotion. And this relationship between words, thinking and emotions is key to why our thinking can so often be flawed.

Words and Emotion
Now while there might be words that have an emotional connotation for almost everyone, for example the word "suicide," each of us will attach a significant emotional meaning to words based on our past experiences. Someone who was attacked, slammed into a lamppost and badly beaten or abused, will have a strong emotional reaction to the words "lamppost."

Actually, I just changed that last sentence. Originally, I wrote:

So, someone who was attacked, *pushed* into a lamppost   and badly beaten or abused…

I changed it from *pushed* to *slammed* because obviously the latter conveys more violence and is thus generates stronger emotion in the reader.

Sticks, Stones and Sensitivity

The Christian Recorder of March 1862, a publication of the African Methodist Episcopal Church, is often mentioned as the first recorded instance of this phrase...

Sticks and stones may break my bones but words will never hurt me

Well, the latest research suggests that this might need to be tweaked a bit:

Sticks and stones may break my bones but words might stimulate an emotional reaction, and who knows where it will go from there.

Of course, not all words have a general emotional meaning but, in theory, *almost every word could not just convey but create some emotion based on a person's experience. A bit like a song that you love, words can turn on the emotion, which leads to a critical part of the "thinking" recipe.*

Words, therefore, are how we articulate our thoughts and communicate ideas and they are emotionally laden. They can connect neurologically to the emotion areas of the brain, creating a significant emotional response.

Metaphors
Now, as words can individually set off emotional responses, eventually humans realized that they could use words to exaggerate and direct the emotional responses of their listeners. And this is precisely what metaphors do. They arouse an emotional response in the listener by association.

Think of it this way.

Words are the message, but it is emotion that energizes them.

For example, if you want to really criticize someone and get sympathy for doing so, you can compare them to Hitler in one way or another. This person is Hitleresque, or their actions remind you of Hitler, who probably is in contemporary memory, the most hated man in the history of the world. Mission achieved, you have connected this person to the emotional associations already in the brain with Hitler.

Now, not every listener going to have that emotional reaction. It can rebound. For example, those who understand what the speaker is trying to do might instead associate them with manipulation and the emotions that go along with that. Heck, they might even call the speaker a "Judas."

There have been numerous studies on how metaphors influence perception and thinking. In one Stanford study, for example, researchers found that how they described criminal activity, influenced the solutions offered by the subjects.

In this 2013 study by Thibodeau and Boroditsky, the researchers used two different metaphors to describe crime. When crime was framed metaphorically as "a virus," subjects proposed social reform initiatives, like eradicating poverty and increasing education. However, when crime was described as a "beast", subjects' solutions were more direct and aggressive, like focusing on catching and jailing criminals.

The Limitation of a Word

Another problem with words is while they help categorize the world and our ideas, they do so in a simplistic way. That is because most words describe a class, without qualification. This works in everyday conversation because we don't need such specification -- or think we do.

"Hey Ma'am," says the cop. "Did you see that car that just sped through here?"

"Yes," says the woman. "It was a blue car."

"Can you provide any more details? We want to ask the driver about a murder."

"Oh, wow. I think it had South Carolina plates."

"Anything else?"

"It was definitely an SUV."

"Anything else?"

"Yes, I think it was a Ford."

"Great. Any more details?"

"It had a sticker on the back fender that said, "Back off."

"That's awesome, ma'am. Anything else?"

"It had a chrome roof rack with a bicycle on top."

"You're being so helpful, Ma'am. Can you think of anything else?"

"I think there were three passengers. One driver, and two people sitting in the back."

"Amazing, ma'am. You know you might get some sort of reward for this."

"Really? Let me think. Oh, I don't think the right taillight was working."

So, it wasn't just a car, it was a blue car. Actually, it was a blue Ford SUV, with South Carolina plates, with a specific sticker on the back, with a chrome roof rack with a black bicycle on top, and a right taillight that was broken and there was a driver and two passengers in the back, according to a female bystander who was questioned at the scene by a police officer who mentioned she might get a reward.

As we have already seen, memory is unreliable and therefore the bystander's description almost certainly has some details wrong.

The point is that increasing levels of description are required to take a word or an idea and thoroughly define it. This has been an issue in philosophy for eons.

There were the *Skeptics* who believed that the search for knowledge or truth is an infinite regress with no end. You just keep digging and digging but never reach an end point.

Then there are the *Stoics* who believe the skeptics go too far and that at some point in the process you have enough understanding for it to be useful.

This balance between continued exploration of an issue and recognizing when the information you have is useful enough for your purposes turns out to be crucial.

Words allow us to manipulate, consciously or otherwise. They frame and fine tune our perceptions, emotions and thus our memories, too. They become the instruments with which we can fool others and ourselves.

One of the endearing things about dogs, cats and other domestic pets – except parrots -- is that they don't speak. Of course, they convey their emotions through facial expressions and physical appearance. If they want something from you, like a treat, dogs might walk up to you and look you lovingly in the eye or emit a soft bark. If they don't get one, most will slowly slink away and go to sleep or play with a toy. But what they definitely don't do is speak as in: "Hey dude! What the hell is wrong with you? Can't you see I want a treat? You're so darned inconsistent. Three out of the last five days you have given me a treat at this time, but on the other two you have just ignored me! You say you love me but I'm beginning to wonder about that!"

It is interesting to speculate about what came first, complex emotions or the words to describe them. Perhaps they came about the same time? No, the emotions surely came first because they seem necessary for survival and adaptation. But what surely preceded words were perceptions. We need to interpret the world to survive; the perceptions are there in one way or another. Words merely articulate them or confound them, or both.

Science and Iceberg Thinking
The reason why research descriptions are, or should be, long winded, is that in the pursuit of accuracy of the evidence, the activity needs to be thoroughly defined.

Here's a hypothetical example. And here's the supposed take away from this hypothetical study.

"Recent research showed that 12% of men are bald."

To really understand how well this statement reflects "reality", you have to qualify almost every word in the sentence.

How recent? Was it 2017 or 1997? The culture around hairstyles has changed over that time period and that is likely to influence the outcome.

Research? Who conducted the research? Where was it conducted? Why did they pursue this research? Was there one research site or many? In one country or several? Did the researchers have any special interests? What was the research paradigm?

Showed? How did it show this? Was it a self-report survey, or did the researchers literally count heads? What statistical methods were used? How reliable are they? What is the margin of error? Who did the analysis?

12%? How many subjects were there in the survey? How was that number calculated?

Men? Which men? What were the ages of the subjects? What were their ethnic backgrounds? Their health status? Where do they live? What were the socio-economic and marital status of the men? How long had they been bald?

Bald? What is the definition of bald? Did some men choose to be bald and others have no options? How many of the non-bald men had undergone hair transplants or used other remedies to restore their hair?

These are only a small sampling of the qualifying questions that would help clarify the "findings." It is why science writing is full of descriptors. To reflect all the main issues, or the ones that we think are important, the study should be reported something like this.

"A study conducted in Siberia, between 1999-2000, surveyed 65 mine workers about their level of baldness. The Study was conducted by the Russian Department of Health and utilized the

BORIS (Baldness Of Rabotnik[9] In Siberia) test, which had previously been validated and shown to have high inter-rater reliability and modest deviation errors. The subjects completed the self-report BORIS questionnaire. A small sample of the participants (n=5), were interviewed face-to-face to establish reliability of the scores. The reliability was high, with 80% of the scores validated. Baldness was defined as "hair has stopped growing for at least a year." Of the original 65 subjects, 15 subjects' responses were eliminated from the final statistics. The study was funded by Vosstanovlenie Volos[10] a private corporation based in Moscow."

If you think that is funny and even absurd, you should know that some research, and particularly its translation into everyday life, like drug trials, is just as error-prone, misleading, and not so funny. For example, the antidepressant drug Prozac was originally approved for use based on a research trial involving just 286 patients, *all men*, using the drug for 6 to 8 weeks. The pill was also supplemented by an anti-anxiety drug. Negative results were also suppressed, and some patients were switched between groups.[11]

How many times have people quoted "research" findings to you, or you have read about them? Do most people delve into the research details or do they just accept the information?

"Get your facts first, then you can distort them as you please."
Mark Twain

Well, for one thing, most people aren't trained in research analysis but in any event, the "finding" may or may not influence anyone coming across it. For example, someone reading about the bald "data" mentioned above, might just dismiss it, but another person

---

[9] Worker in Russian
[10] Hair Restoration Inc.
[11] The Sedated Society

might decide to get into the hair restoration business because of the purportedly high percentage of bald guys.

The problem with this hypothetical study is that there are far too few subjects and indeterminate reliability to draw any useful conclusions. Moreover, there was a vested interest of the funding agency which also suggests lack of independence, so we have to call this study pseudoscience (see chapter 16). However, as we shall see, that doesn't prevent it from being treated like a proven reality and influencing people's views about the prevalence of baldness.

There is a later chapter about science and research that explores this topic more and shows, despite all of these qualifications, researchers are human and still subject to the main biases of the mind. Nonetheless, the main point here is that in order to attempt to get closer to the truth, we have to keep qualifying our concepts. And each level of qualification comes with its own limitations. For example, in the case of the runaway car conversation above, a blue car is better than a car with no description of color, but the next question is *what color* blue?

Iceberg Thinking
Carl Jung, the great explorer of the mind and the subconscious, termed the phrase "iceberg thinking" to refer to the fact that consciousness was at the tip of the mental iceberg, but that underneath, there was a vast unconscious that also contributed to thought, emotions and behavior.

I use the term differently. I use it to refer to the unpeeling back of the layers of an idea or thought, so it can be better understood and qualified. I believe that is an essential cognitive and life skill that is most effectively taught in science, but I'll leave that for a later chapter. The fact is that the deep dive below the surface is necessary to get closer to the 'truth.'

You might think that this level of qualification is only necessary when talking about science and research. No! Far from it.

"Hey, Jan, did you hear about Fiona? She was arrested for shoplifting last night!"

"Oh, No! Really? I can't believe it. Where is she?" responds Fiona's best friend Sue.

"I think she might still be in jail. Not sure."

"We must get to see her right away! This is terrible. I'm heartbroken," says Sue stifling back the tears.

Reality check: Fiona was shopping with her mother. As they were leaving, the alarm went off. The security guard came over and checked her mother's receipt. After a brief interview, it was discovered that a pack of kitchen towels in the bottom of her cart hadn't been rung up. Fiona's mother duly paid for them and she and her daughter left the store.

The derivation of this piece of fake news, is that someone heard about Fiona being stopped and interrogated by a security guard for shoplifting. *If you stop there and don't get beyond the surface of the iceberg*, it can lead almost anywhere, including the supposition that Fiona has been arrested and is in jail.

In other words, given even the smallest amount of information, our imaginations run wild.

"But Howard, we can't spend our time analyzing everything we read and everything people tell us. There'd be no time to do anything else."

That's probably true. But the point is that even if you don't have the time for critical thinking, or think you don't, *it's essential to recognize the limitations of words and ideas and how they reflect reality.* Moreover, you do need to make time for the deep dive in the important areas of your life if you want those decisions to be as fully informed as possible. It won't be perfect, but it'll be better than a superficial scan of the top of the iceberg. You have to make the conscious effort, or you will be driven by whim, false assumptions and the views of others.

"So, Doc, you're telling me I have to think and act like Captain Spock? I have to be rational about every damn thing? We all know how much fun he was!"

Well, on some things, yes and other things, no. Sometimes you have to dig into the iceberg and sometimes you don't. Sometimes you can be stoic and sometimes a skeptic.

Wife: Where do you want to go for dinner tonight? Italian or Japanese??

Husband: Well, it depends. As for the Italian place, it can be crowded at this time on a Wednesday evening. I do like their wine, though. However, their sauces can vary in quality and if you recall, one time, I had to return the pasta. On the other hand, I am going to run in the morning so loading up on carbs wouldn't be a bad thing. It also depended on whether our favorite waitress is on tonight: she's the best.

Wife: So, is that a yes or no to the Italian restaurant?

Husband: Well, let me consider the alternative. The sushi is great at the Japanese place, but it depends on whether that chef is on the schedule tonight. The others are not so good at making their special roll we love so much. Also, it's a slightly longer drive and the forecast was for rain to start in about twenty minutes. It would be good if we got that seat by the window, but that's generally reserved. Also, it's a little more expensive than the Italian restaurant although I think it's probably better value.

Wife: Just tell me! Italian or Japanese???

Husband: I need to think about this a little more. What do we plan on doing after we have eaten? I generally feel a little fuller after the Italian meal, and also, we don't have alcohol when we go to the Japanese restaurant. Hmm. Also, it still might be raining when we get out so that might affect what we do.

Wife: Just f****** make up your mind!

Husband: Well, it's not that easy. I guess the question is whether I want to emphasize the entire eating experience or the food. After all, the ambience is definitely better at the Italian restaurant....

Wife: Screw it. I'm making myself a sandwich.

On the other hand, here's a conversation between two young adults.

Guy: Wow, you're awesome. I know we've only been dating a few weeks but the sex is amazing. Will you marry me?

Girl: Yes!!!

Asking more questions to dive as far as possible into an issue is very important in some things, and totally unnecessary in others. However, you have to know how to do the deep dive and when to do it, otherwise you'll be making poorly informed decisions that will affect the rest of your life and probably other people's lives, too.

What you have to ask yourself as you face any decision is how important is the decision and how will the outcome affect your life? The amount of digging you do depends on how important the decision really is.

Later, we will see that this iceberg thinking is almost a reflexive, automatic response for many people in which case it might be better called "Kneejerk" thinking -- with the emphasis on the jerk.

This is amplified when we consider *the backfire effect,* the tendency for people *to harden* in their beliefs when they are presented with contrary information.

The characterization and separation of the world through words also leads to another big problem: The simplistic division of the world.

Questions
1. When you see a fact quoted or mentioned by someone else, how deep do you go to check out its validity?
2. Have you ever discovered that an important piece of information conveyed to you was essentially incorrect? How did you react? How often does that happen?
3. What factors would lead you to unconditionally accept a piece of information?
4. How quickly do you make important decisions?

Chapter Six

The Binary Brain and Determinism

Yogi Berra was a baseball great, a catcher who played for the famous New York Yankees. Berra garnered almost as much attention off the field as he did on it by saying things that sounded ridiculous and illogical. He became the poster child for absurdity. However, some of his sayings that made people laugh, aren't irrational -- they are testament to how fixed we are in our thinking.

In the last chapter, we looked at the evolution of language and the use of words. As soon as you create a word for something it becomes a separate and distinct concept that is highlighted -- and perceived -- by its difference rather than its overlap with other ideas. Take the concepts of mind and body, the physical and psychological. As you think about those concepts, they seem independent and separate, but they are not. Although they exist as independent *concepts* they are not independent in reality, influencing each other by varying degrees in different situations. Berra famously said:

"Baseball is 90% mental and the other half is physical."

It is easy when we hear that to laugh and claim that it's just Yogi being Yogi. However, that is only the case if you believe that the physical and psychological are separate, independent entities. If they are not independent entities, then it is possible that their various contributions exceed 100%. If psychology contributes to physical performance as well as to psychological factors, then it indeed can be 90% and physical factors 50%.

On another occasion someone asked Yogi what time it was.

"You mean right now?" Yogi replied, proving that he was a genius who understood parallel universes, relativity and the space-time continuum better than most catchers in the American League.

The brain's tendency to seek separation in a world of inter-connection is called *the binary brain*. It is so much easier to divide things into either/or rather than either/and. It is far less effort, for example, to think of a disease as either physical or psychological rather than both.

Not only do we have to contend with overlapping concepts, we then have to weight each one's contribution, and that is very often an extremely daunting task.

This tendency towards simplicity has been reinforced because some of the time, reducing an explanation to one concept works and it certainly saves energy and time.

For example, treating tuberculosis as a purely physical condition allowed numerous effective treatments to be implemented in the nineteenth century. However, typically a binary brain solution works initially but to progress beyond a certain point, requires more expansive thinking and a deeper dive. Thus, the famous nineteenth century physician William Osler is quoted as saying that "the treatment of tuberculosis depends more on what the patient has in his mind than he does on his chest." Osler was a thought leader who saw the limitations of a purely physical approach to disease and medicine in general.

By artificially dividing reality into separate, mutually distinct concepts, the binary brain creates a limitation on the thought process. Seeing beyond these limitations and being open to a more complex construction of events is the heart of creativity and "thinking outside the box." The binary brain is the box.

The binary brain also sets us up for bigotry and discrimination.

The combination of focusing on differences rather than similarities and the overlap between two concepts, PLUS the difficulty of weighting different individual contributions to the whole, means that the brain's default setting is to completely overvalue separateness and difference. For example, despite the fact that all humans are at least 99.5% the same genetically, we divide each other way more than we see our similarities. Part of the reason for this is that the brain works on contrast. It looks for ways to discriminate between stimuli, concepts and impressions and then overvalues those differences as a result. What this means is that we have to make a very conscious effort to avoid stereotyping and accepting and overvaluing simplistic binary brain perceptions.

The problem is that simple binary thinking works a lot of the time. Think about the internal conversation you might have about what to have for dinner.

First, you think of several alternatives but quickly you narrow the choice down to two. Why? Because trying to make a choice out of five possibilities is way too difficult. You would have to make at least 10 comparisons of the different meals. You quickly switch into binary mode.

Now, that may seem like an adaptive tactic but there's actually a big problem with it.

You are training your brain to seek binary simplicity.

Fast forward to a different scenario. As an HR manager, you have to make a decision between two candidates. Of course, you have narrowed the list down to two not five because it's so much easier to compare two people. The *contrast effect* highlights the tendency to see the differences rather than the similarities between two things when compared side by side, whereas when compared with several others, you are more likely to see their similarities. Indeed, you have used that process to narrow down the list.

Now the differences between the two candidates will stand out, no matter whether those differences are relevant or not to their ability to be effective employees.

One of the differences might be skin color. One person is yellow and the other person is blue. This is where you have to be really critical and careful.

Your brain seeing this skin color difference will then automatically present you with all the notions you have about yellow people and blue people. Some of these ideas you might not actually believe or even have thought about much, let alone validated. This is an example of *the group attribution error*, the biased belief that the characteristics of an individual group member are reflective of the group as a whole. In other words, all blue people are the same. You have to work hard not only to be conscious of these stereotypes but to actually fight them in your head.

Hopefully, future generations will be in disbelief that people were once discriminated on grounds of the color of the body's largest organ – the skin. Probably some discerning children of the future will ask, "Back in the twenty-first century did they also discriminate based on the size of someone's kidney or the shape of their liver?"

It turns out that the brain and the human mind are much more interested in simplicity and easy stereotypes than complexity. Rationality is hard work and besides, most people aren't trained in logical and statistical analysis. In fact, we have to switch into a completely different thinking mode to perform that deep rational analysis. There are many different shortcuts that we take to ensure we don't have to do the hard, and energy consuming work, of the deep rational analysis. And they set us up for creating stereotypes – absurdly simple and dangerously false.

Once you understand the many different forms of these shortcuts, called "cognitive bias," you will see them everywhere -- hopefully most of all in yourself. And you'll see that by and large thinking isn't good for you. Okay, that's a bit extreme, but you'll see that the human mind is actually not that good at accurately predicting behavior and making rational decisions. (However, in some ways thinking isn't good for you. For example, in an upcoming book *The Pain Mindset* military physical therapist Major Jeff Frankart presents a very plausible case for the argument that when we expect pain, the brain delivers it. When you train people to not expect pain, they don't experience it. Thinking can indeed create real problems.)

I am not talking about getting test answers correct or solving math or closed end problems. Of course, you can be right in answering a crossword clue, a question of arithmetic or a matter of fact. Life, however, is not a math quiz. Even within the material world and certainly outside it, life is full of vague shapes and multiple shades of grey, all open to interpretation. And it is this interpretative process that makes us who we are; creative, imaginative -- and flawed.

The Material World and Certainty
The problem is that the elements of the material world aren't like people. They don't have choice and can't talk themselves into anything. For example, if water had a human brain, any molecule of it might say, "I'm bored today. I am going to boil at 165 degrees because I can't be bothered to wait until it reaches 212." Imagine the chaos that would create.

Because the elements of the material world tend to act consistently, although not without uncertainty, we still view them with certainty. And that introduces the concept of determinism, that *a causes b* and the world is full of certainties. The binary brain loves determinism because it is simplistic. Because of the binary brain it is easy to think of determinism in terms of certainties than mere probabilities. Which brings us nicely to Descartes and the Reformation, where the binary brain arbitrarily divided the world between mind and body, setting western thought back centuries.

Even Shakespeare got it wrong

"To be or not to be" is NOT the question. That's just an example of the binary brain reducing existence to over-simplistic polar alternatives.

Nearly three hundred years ago, Thomas Bayes annoyed the scientific establishment by suggesting that phenomena needed to be seen as probabilities that vary as more data are acquired; indeterminate, and by implication, they could not be the basis of inviolable laws. The notion of universal truths was dealt a big blow, but we still tend to think in terms of certainties rather than probabilities.

Today, Bayesian ideas are widely accepted, especially in the light of the research demonstrating cognitive bias. We think of facts as 100% accurate when for the most part they are probabilities that are bounded by many, often unknown, variables. And this is a significant problem, especially in medicine and healthcare, where prognoses are often delivered as certainties when they are in fact probabilities. If you are told you are going to die within three years, and believe it, you probably will.

However, even when we, at some level, realize that much of our factual evidence is really a probability, we still often think of it as a certainty.

This becomes a problem, especially in life or death issues.

A neighbor of mine was having some health issues and went to her local doctor for some tests. When they came back, the doctor pronounced, correctly, that there was a 95% chance that there was really nothing to worry about. There had been a concern that her symptoms might even reflect cancer.

What would you do? 95% odds of the problem being benign sound pretty good.

My neighbor wanted more certainty and that meant having a procedure at the state center of excellence, The Medical University of South Carolina, MUSC, in Charleston.

When she came round from the procedure the surgeon came by to chat.

"You're one lucky woman," the surgeon pronounced. "We have found early stage cancer in your pancreas."

That was seven years ago and my neighbor is in remission. Had she not followed up, she probably wouldn't be here any longer.

Note that her primary care physician was right; the tests showed that there was a 95% chance that nothing was seriously wrong.

However, *the default position is still to see probabilistic facts as certainties,* which then allows us to divide the world into black and white. Yes or no. Either one thing or the other.

We welcome that certainty, because it gives us clarity, but we overvalue it because we think it gives us clarity.

Do you think that binary thinking leads to absurd simplicity? Yes or No?

Let's take a current example: vaccinations.

In most cases, vaccinations will help a significant percentage of people. The CDC estimate that flu shots actually prevent the flu in about 50% of the people who get them. Most of the remainder experience no effects whatsoever from the flu shot.

However, let's suppose there's a vaccination that prevents a childhood illness. It's effective in say 60% of cases, has no effect on 35% of people, has mildly negative effects on 3% of people but potentially serious effects on 2% of children. Seems pretty safe, but it's not perfect. What would you do?

It would be so much easier if there was a zero chance of negative side-effects but in this hypothetical example it doesn't, so you have to make the choice for your child.

Now, from a parent's perspective, this is a dilemma. From a public health official's perspective there is no dilemma, because from a public health point of view the vaccinations have overwhelmingly positive results. It's not as simple as a yes or no response. The public health worker is not that concerned about a rare high risk, but of course, the parents very much are.

We create our world through a binary lens. For example, when we watch team sports games, like soccer, we have two teams playing against each other, facing each other from opposite ends of the field. However, if we represented reality, or at least a deep dive into a topic, this is metaphorically like watching ten teams play against each other on the same field. Imagine how confusing that would be!

Those other ten teams would reflect some of the variables that influence an outcome which, in human studies at the very least would be genetics, socio-economic status, macro-culture, family "values", nutrition, exercise, sleep, stress, stress management, microculture (the social circle), numerous health parameters, etc. etc.

In addition, there would be another twenty teams playing that we couldn't even see! These are the yet to be discovered variables, that will be revealed in the future, like…. Well, we'll have to wait for the future to find out what they are.

It's all so confusing, that we end up cherry-picking those aspects of "reality" that we are more emotionally comfortable with (see Politics).

The truth is rarely pure and never simple -- Oscar Wilde

The material world does offer us hard and fast laws that are tough to contradict. You may choose not to believe in gravity but you are likely to soon be brought down to earth. As Kahneman implies, the most logical many of us are each day is when we turn the door handle the right way to open it. And of course, some cats and dogs do that, too. However, we want the apparent deterministic certainty of the material world to apply to everything because it is neat, tidy, and more importantly, gives us a sense of control.

But when we step out of the material world, we run into trouble. However, because the physical world forces us to accept some fundamental laws and logic, the generalization of those principles to the non-physical world falls flat. We continue with the *pretense* of rationality.

You can't blame gravity for falling in love -- Albert Einstein

Our minds are designed to be blind to these failings. We need to have some organizing principles to make us feel we have some measure of control. If we face the reality that we are very simplistic, biased creatures who work on stereotypes, naive assumptions, and narcissistic perceptions, we would be undermined and bereft. It's better to feel that we are occasionally wrong than completely lost. It's hard for us to accept that our thought process is flawed.

We're blind to our blindness. We have very little idea of how little we know. We're not designed to know how little we know.
--Daniel Kahneman

Of course, one of the problems of disseminating the view that our thinking is flawed is that by definition, the theory itself is flawed! However, I defer here to the British statistician George Box who famously said:

"Essentially, all models are wrong, some are useful." -- George Box

Of course, he was talking about scientific models not runway superstars. Essentially, however, all thoughts are wrong, some are useful. Wrong in the sense that we classify most sense impressions very simplistically and judge them the same way. This is the *Stoic* position: the data might not be perfect, but they still have usefulness.

Another problem contributing to binary perception is that the brain works on **contrast** and therefore the more contrasted sensory input and concepts are, the more we notice the difference and the easier it becomes to make distinctions and decisions. Hence the binary brain that likes to see stark contrasts rather than shades of grey. Fifty shades of grey might inspire titillating interest as a book or movie but in reality, trying to attribute a scale that has fifty gradations of a concept would drive most people bonkers. It is extremely difficult to weight different concepts in the same way that we can assign formulas in the physical world. Which is why we don't do it and stick to simplistic binary divisions -- like Democrat or Republican.

There is speculation about when binary thinking develops. Have you ever said to a three-year old, "You can have the cookies or the ice-cream?" The likely reply is "Why can't I have both?"

Perhaps this is just a sign of a greedy kid. Or perhaps it's just a sign of someone who doesn't think in a binary way. Why can't he or she have both? Being forced to choose between one or another is an arbitrary binary distinction imposed by an adult and not a reflection of the child's reality.

When you combine these three aspects of mental functioning: the automatic narrative created by two associated ideas, the assumption that they are causally related, and a binary perception, we get into big problems.

For example, in a recent newspaper piece, the writer who penned a story about a guy, said that he had broken off a relationship with a woman. The writer then added without further qualification, "The woman committed suicide 12 years later."

The reflexive response of many readers will now be to associate the man with the woman's suicide. This reflexive narrative may come with some emotion, like anger at the man for effectively "killing" someone. We create the narrative out of two ideas, often the only two "facts" we know and then connect them causally. It takes some training and effort to recognize that conclusion is based on reflexive, default brain function not the truth. It's kneejerk thinking. It's fake news.

However, this is now the underlying principle of much communication, including "news." We have learnt that we can influence others, and maybe a lot of people, using this *false association method* that takes advantage of the mind's narrative process. And, given what we have learned about words, those who are wordsmiths can even more effectively get the response they want in their audience.

Inbuilt cognitive biases allow us to shape narratives that are broadly consistent with each other. We are story-telling machines who are more interested in 'cognitive ease,' than rational analysis; more geared to internal consistency than the truth, our perceptions rather than reality. Logic and rationality don't have much to do with it, sometimes even in science, where you would expect logic to prevail.

The cognitive research also shows that thinking is often flawed and much more influenced by emotion than rationality. Antonio Damasio's classic book *Descartes Error* highlighted the fact that the distinction between emotion and rationality is far too simplistic and that emotions and 'somatic markers' – physical sensations -- influence thought, too. And this turns out to be a huge piece of the puzzle.

"The truth is an ambition which is beyond us." – Peter Ustinov

Questions
1. Do you recognize when arguments are presented in a binary way?
2. If you challenge people on the binary nature of their arguments, what happens?
3. Do you recognize when you are using binary thinking?
4. What questions do you need to ask yourself when confronted with a binary argument?

Chapter Seven

Emotions and Thoughts

Emotion is a wonderful thing – or can be. It can inspire great artistic works and drive people to amazing feats of courage. The problem is it can also be used to fuel mass murder, satanic evil and unimaginable crimes. It can inspire Mozart, but it can also inspire terrorists. Accepting narratives based only on emotion is a slippery slope that potentially leads to disaster on a mass scale and the erosion of rational principles.

When emotion replaces reason as a basis of judgment, perception and behavior, any individual, no matter how insane, is empowered to justify any behavior whatsoever.

Social norms are at risk of disappearing and the society becomes incredibly narcissistic. Truth is sacrificed for animal instincts. The Lower Power prevails. Would you trust a gorilla with nuclear weapons?

However, the role of emotion is even more complex.

The New England Patriots, Manchester United and the Neural Basis of Thought

Do you support a sports team? If you do, you're probably more loyal to it than anything else in your life, even your spouse. I mean, how many people divorce their sports teams? The term "lifelong" fan is redundant. If you're a fan, you have been and will almost certainly continue to be a fan until your dying day. Your team can lose way more games than they win, they can trade your favorite players, they can charge astronomical prices for a hot dog, they can cheat, they can hire front office staff with the morals of Satan, but you will still support them forever. Fans will do almost anything for their team, even go to war for them. Moreover, you might not be able to recall what you're meant to do today, the date you got married, or even your kid's birthday but you'll vividly recall all the great moments you have witnessed in your team's history. Boy, if you had this sort of commitment when you were going through the education system, you'd be an Emeritus Professor by now.

What is it about the New England Patriots, Manchester Uniteds or any favorite sports team that can turn any of us into totally committed supercharged geniuses on the subject of our team? In a word -- emotion. Most sports are emotional roller coasters. For the ninety minutes of a soccer game involving your favorite team, your brain is fired up, literally and metaphorically. Neurotransmitters, especially serotonin and dopamine, swamp your brain increasing attention, memory and basically supercharging it. The feeling is naturally addictive -- even if your team is losing. There's a reason why we're called fans -- short for fanatics. Your brain is on fire, passionately engaged, in interpreting the action.

This level of emotion not only makes you super attentive on match day, enhancing your focus and memory, it *also creates neural structures that underpin your very thought processes*. For example, you'll be more attentive to and attracted by information about your team. You will see all the refereeing errors that go against your team and hardly any that go for them, unless they're really blatant and then, of course, you'll say your team deserves a break because of all the poor decisions that always go against them. When you see other fans acting exactly the same way for their teams, you'll call them irrational and blind idiots. The team can become so much of your identity that you will buy clothes and other items to highlight your connection with them. You might even name your children after one or more of their players. If Descartes had said, "I am a sports fan, therefore I am," he might have been onto something.

The level of emotion that accompanies your experience of following your favorite sports teams turns you into a biased, irrational addict with an extreme level of commitment. If you were this committed to your eating and exercise program, you'd be so healthy, it would be sickening. You'd probably live to 140.

The sports fan analogy is extreme, but it shows the role of emotion in shaping our thoughts and experience. The question is how much more rational, if at all, are we in other areas of our lives? Just like the addict's brain creates a neural structure that supports seeking, justifying and prioritizing drug use, emotion can turn us into irrational and biased creatures with an inability to be discerning and rational about our own -- or anyone else's -- behavior. And I haven't even ventured into politics, yet. Of course, political affiliation is basically the same process.

YGOWYPI!
The principle here is very simple: **Y**ou **G**et **O**ut **W**hat **Y**ou **P**ut **I**n. When you're cheering on your team you are setting up your neurology to be totally committed to it in everything you do. You're training your brain that your team is your priority and pretty much everything else is secondary. Whenever we act, especially when emotion is involved, we're building brain structures to support those actions. Your undying fervent and emotional support trains and shapes your thought process.

Let me introduce you to my English Setter Jack.

I'll admit that sometimes I feed my sweet and loving dog, scraps from the table. However, when guests come to dinner and he starts nuzzling them at the table I go ballistic.

"Bad dog, Jack!" I yell, "Leave Joe alone!"

Of course, I am completely to blame. I have trained Jack to come to the table looking for food and I'm being totally irrational if I expect him not to do so. I have trained his brain to expect scraps from the table. The fact that I only do this sometimes simply reinforces this more -- what B.F. Skinner fans will know as the *power of intermittent reinforcement.* Intermittent reinforcement is more powerful than continuous reinforcement, because it is less predictable -- reward doesn't happen every time -- so we persist more. That is why when our team loses it actually makes us more committed. I mean who would want to support a team that won every game in a landslide? Or put it another way, supporting a team that was totally dominant would be a different experience. For one thing, the expectation that they would win and win big, would likely modulate the emotion of watching the game and thus the experience.

Anyway, your brain is like my dog -- it will do what you have trained it to do. What you get out is what you have put in. Incidentally, this mechanism means that our pets, especially those who have been with us from their birth, are going to reflect us because we have been shaping their brains with our behavior. There really is no esoteric mystery here; it's just a matter of training.

"Insanity is training your brain to do the same thing over and over again and expecting it to act differently." -- modified Einstein quote.

A great example of the confusion created by the binary brain is the distinction between thoughts and emotions. They are separate concepts but it turns out that they are way more interconnected than the binary distinction implies.

If you look at the anatomy of the brain, you can see that there are four vertical levels broadly related to evolutionary development.

At the bottom of the vertical scale is the Brainstem. In general, this controls many basic, automatic and unconscious functions, such as breathing and involuntary movements.

Above the Brainstem is the Midbrain, which coordinates a lot of sensory processing and passes that information up the structure of the brain.

Above the Midbrain is the Limbic System, which is heavily involved in emotional responses, attention, the formation of memory and control of the flight/fight autonomic system.

Above the Limbic System is the Cerebral Cortex, where more sophisticated processes of thinking, planning and execution are managed.

There are many interconnecting parts of the brain, with informational highways passing critical data from one area to others. For example, the limbic system connects with the cerebral cortex and vice-versa.

The assumption is that dominance works from the lower level of the primitive functions in the brainstem, up to the top. At times of stress, for example, there is an automatic and rapid change in functions at the brainstem, midbrain and limbic levels. Breathing and metabolism increase, sending hormones through the body, the limbic system sends alarm signals throughout the brain and initially, at least, these actions overwhelm the cerebral cortex who can only be aware of the changes but helpless to do much about them, at least in the first few milliseconds that they occur.

After a short period of time, the cortex can exert some analysis of the situation and possibly change the emotional reaction. With training and practice we can also train the cortex to exert more control on lower functions by, for example, deep breathing to slow down heart rate and the escalation of the stress response.

This complex system then goes into action first and asks questions later. Survival is too critical to be left to cortical interference, at least initially. We react and then analyze. The problem is that reactions and analyses are not separate, unrelated entities. The thought process is likely to be different if you are relaxed than when you are stressed. In other words, emotion will influence perception. However, perceptions also influence emotions.

For example, suppose you find yourself in a room with some other people and you start to notice that your body and senses seem to be energized. Your heart seems to be beating faster, and you feel as if you're almost sweating. How do you interpret these perceived changes?

Perhaps you're feeling the symptoms of some germ or bug?

Perhaps your anxiety has just increased because of something that happened in the room?

Perhaps someone just turned up the heating?

Perhaps you realize that you have a huge crush on the guy/girl sitting next to you and they are about to engage you in conversation?

How you initially interpret those physiological sensations will impact your perception, the developing narrative and your behavior.

If you think that your feelings might be part of attraction, you might well then seek justification for being thus attracted. Which could then lead to a cascade of thought about how great that other person really is. This could lead anywhere and all because you're getting a cold!

Which makes you wonder how many people's initial infatuation and even subsequent marriage was based on a virus? Love bug indeed!

Lisa Barrett is a research psychologist whose excellent book *How Emotions Are Made* sheds some very important light on the processing of emotions and thinking.

When you were reading about the brain and the infrastructure that underpins emotions, it was no doubt tempting to see the complex, interconnecting brain structures as *responsible* for emotion. But what does "responsible for" mean?

Yes, these structures provide the hardware, not just for emotions, but for almost everything that happens to you. However, that doesn't mean they are necessarily *responsible for* them any more than your stove is responsible for the meal you just cooked.

The classical view of emotions was that they are inbuilt and unwavering expressions of each emotion that manifest themselves the same in everybody. For example, anxiety is associated with an increase in heart rate, certain facial expressions and other bodily postures. Joy is always experienced by the same internal feelings, powered by neurochemicals like oxytocin and dopamine and characterized by smiles and an energized posture. Moreover, because we are all human being everyone feels, and manifests, these emotions in the same way.

Barrett debunks this view. Her research as well as that of others shows that emotion doesn't quite work this way. In fact, there isn't a universal expression of these emotions. Different cultures express emotions quite differently, through the words they use and the expressions that accompany those feelings.

Barrett writes:

"Not all cultures understand emotions as internal mental states. Himba and Hadza emotion concepts, for example, appear to be more focused on   actions. This is also true of certain Japanese emotion concepts. The Ifaluk of Micronesia consider emotions as transactions between people. To them, anger is not a feeling of rage, a scowl, a pounding fist, or a loud yelling voice, all within the skin of one person, but a situation in which two people are engaged in a script—a dance, if you will—around a common goal. In the Ifaluk view, anger does not "live" inside either participant." (p 53)

"Your familiar emotion concepts are built-in only because you grew up in a particular social context where those emotion concepts are meaningful and useful, and your brain applies them outside your awareness to construct your experiences. Heart rate changes are inevitable; their emotional meaning is not." (p.33)

Even more importantly, the personal expression of emotions varies from occasion to occasion. If you're angry on two occasions the expression of your anger is likely to vary, influenced by many factors, like the context you're in, the people you're around and so on.

Milton Erickson is arguably one of the greatest psychiatrists and psychotherapists ever. He recognized that rational conversation about change would often arouse anxiety within the client and this would feed back negatively on the whole perception of change. However, what if the discussion about critical personal change didn't arouse anxiety?

Great, but how do you achieve that?

Well, one method that Erickson used was to change the perception of the "anxiety." He would sometimes have his patients running on the spot as they discussed these sensitive issues. The patient's heart rate would indeed go up, but was attributed to the exercise they were doing, not the discussion they were having!

The key point here is that your perception and thought process will determine how you label and explain the physical feelings.

I came across a story about a guru who was teaching a pupil meditation. During the meditation, the student opened his eyes and noticed his teacher's expressions alternating between what he perceived as anger and laughter.

When the session was over, the student hesitantly reported his perception to the master.

"Yes, you're right," said the guru, "I was laughing at my anger."

In other words, he could detach from his emotions enough to look at them rather than just feel them. When he did so, he saw his anger as laughable.

This is an interesting exercise. Next time you feel a strong emotion, can you detach yourself from it and see it as something separate from you? And if you can, how do you react to your reaction?

William James proposed that our incredibly varied emotional experiences are constructed from common ingredients. "Emotional brain processes," he wrote, "not only resemble the ordinary sensorial brain-processes, but in very truth are nothing but such processes variously combined."

Barrett comments:
"In the 1960s, the psychologists Stanley Schachter and Jerome Singer famously injected test subjects with adrenaline—without the subjects' knowledge—and saw them experience this mysterious arousal as anger or euphoria, depending on the perceived context." (p. 34).

Recent research on this topic suggests that emotions aren't an automatic brain response to a perceived situation.

As Barrett writes:
"Not every theory agrees on every assumption, but together they assert that emotions are made, not triggered; emotions are highly variable, without fingerprints; and emotions are not, in principle, distinct from cognitions and perceptions." (p. 34).

While the overall infrastructure of the brain is predetermined, the microstructure is dependent on, and shaped by, individual experiences. And those experiences have a huge influence on future perceptions, thoughts and narratives.

Barrett continues;
"The theory of constructed emotion incorporates elements of all three flavors of construction. From social construction, it acknowledges the importance of culture and concepts. From psychological construction, it considers emotions to be constructed by core systems in the brain and body. And from neuro-construction, it adopts the idea that experience wires the brain. (p.35)."

"Rather than assuming there is one universal expression of each key emotion, the theory of constructed emotion, suggests that they are not inborn or universal. The universality exists in "our ability to form concepts, which make our physical sensations meaningful.""

"Social reality is not just about words—it gets under your skin. If you perceive the same baked good as a decadent "cupcake" or a healthful "muffin," research suggests that your body metabolizes it differently. Likewise, the words and concepts of your culture help to shape your brain wiring and your physical changes during emotion."

"Emotions do not shine forth from the face nor from the maelstrom of your body's inner core. They don't issue from a specific part of the brain. No scientific innovation will miraculously reveal a biological fingerprint of any emotion. That's because our emotions aren't built-in, waiting to be revealed. They are made. By us. We don't recognize emotions or identify emotions: we construct our own emotional experiences, and our perceptions of others' emotions, on the spot, as needed, through a complex interplay of systems." (p.40)

The Brain is an Amoral Computer

Whenever we think or act, we are training our brains, even if we are not aware that we are doing that. In doing so, we are also training our unconscious, those processes beyond conscious recognition. Thus, we are unconsciously training our unconscious.

A key issue here is unlike us, or maybe like us, our brains don't make moral distinctions. They do what we have programmed them to do. If there's a moral monitor at all, it's because we have trained the brain to factor it into the equation.

Moreover, our brains don't make the distinction between imagination and reality. How could they? They would need to be fed input about what 'reality' really is, something we are currently unable to do. This process means that once we input something into to our brain, like visualizing, or even thinking about an action, it exists almost as much as a real experience.

This is one reason why we can so easily be tempted and seduced by our own thoughts and it can be difficult to resist temptation. For example, a teenager might be exposed to the idea of snorting cocaine. Part of the teenager knows this is a dumb idea that can only lead to trouble, but in the brain the idea is associated with feelings of excitement and even pleasure. The idea is now energized enough to become a reality, despite the teenager's best intentions and understanding of the dangers, which are hampered by the fact that full development of the frontal lobe typically doesn't develop until one's mid-twenties. (See the **Restraint Bias** in Chapter 11).

Berating someone, particularly young people, for their lack of self-control, or lack of anything isn't an effective strategy. It would be far better to teach them about how the mind works and to give them tools to manage their consciousness (see the How Not To Think workbook at the back of the book).   This bring us conveniently to offendology and political correctness.

Questions
1. Do you always experience your emotions the same way? For example, when you're angry do you always feel, think and act the same way?
2. How accurate are you at reading other people's emotions?
3. What influences your perception of emotion?

Chapter Eight

Offendology and Political Correctness

In the last chapter, I explored the notion that emotions are culturally influenced but individually constructed. They are your *personal response* to a situation.

You probably have said many times something to the effect that...

"...that person makes me so angry!"

However, that is a misconception. Your emotions are constructed by you, not anyone else. Other people may **try** to make you angry, but whether you get angry or not is your choice. Let me say that again...

Your emotions are your choice

Actually, you have two choices. The first is whether you have an emotion, and the second is what to do with it when you do have it.

"C'mon, Doc, there are many people out there who are very annoying! You're telling me I shouldn't react?"

Your emotions, in this case probably anger, are a sign of your discomfort, a warning that something is bothering you. However, once the alarm bell rings, you turn it off and then you *respond* to the situation with adaptive behavior, not uncontrolled emotion.

"Anybody can become angry - that is easy, but to be angry with the right person and to the right degree and at the right time and for the right purpose, and in the right way - that is not within everybody's power and is not easy." -- Aristotle

If you are going to let emotion control your behavior, you won't be very adaptive, and you will only be contributing to narcissism and extremism. And political correctness.

A teacher tells her class of 5th graders that one of the most important things for them to understand is that life is not fair.

A couple of the kids are upset at this and tell their parents.

The parents get angry that the teacher has upset their kids. The parents claim that teaching life isn't fair is unfair and write to the local newspaper with a demand that the teacher in question be fired. There is a school board meeting in which emotions run high. The teacher is put on leave while an investigation is held.

You can get angry about anything you set your mind to. However, it's your mind, and your emotions are based on your specific history and experience. They may not be reflective of other people's views or emotions. The issue here is not the emotion, but what underpins it? Is there any justification for the anger because *it's the reason for the anger that is the issue **not the anger itself.***

Regardless of anyone's feelings the issue in this case is the *appropriateness of the teacher's comments, not someone's emotional reaction to it.*

Is it appropriate to tell 11 year-old kids not to expect life to be fair?

Absolutely. It is a crucial life lesson.

The fact that a parent or whomever, gets upset about it, is not a valid reason for accusing the teacher of anything. Their emotion is a function of their individual experience. And we can say again that sometimes, *Emotions not typical.* Or more accurately in this case, *emotions not justified.*

It's not our emotional responses that are important, it is whether *they are generally appropriate given the circumstances.*

If the issue with the teacher in this example was that she had indulged in some derogatory racial stereotyping, then anger and criticism would be justified. However, the emotion still isn't the issue. The issue would be that a teacher is being harmful by spreading false information. We may be angry, but it isn't the anger that is crucial or even important, *it's the objective judgment that she is having a negative effect on her pupils.*

The problem with political correctness is that it is often based on people's feelings of being offended. But being offended is an individually biased response to a personal perception, which may not be shared by others or even a majority of people. Just being offended isn't an argument. You may justly have a case or you may not, but it is the case that is crucial not your emotions about it.

An emotion is a constructed feeling. It's a physical sensation.

"Doc, I am rejecting your argument because I feel uncomfortable about it," I can hear you say.

"Well, I am rejecting yours because I have indigestion," I reply.

We are both basing our "arguments" or "positions" on physical feelings.

The notion that you have control over your emotions is incredibly empowering.

Think of all those annoying people in your life. Suppose you had enough control to refuse to take the emotional bait. Suppose you refused to be intimidated, angered, frustrated – just think how angry they would get!

I know that emotional control is not easy, but it definitely can be learned. I believe it is crucial for our survival. However, look at the culture today. More and more it is based on emotional manipulation and sensationalism, often for the benefit of the media. Political debates aren't debates, they are more like reality shows with candidates vying to make an emotional impact with a clever one liner. It's designed first and foremost to be entertainment and good for media ratings. Is that how you would choose someone to run your company let alone a country?

Being a slave to emotions is even more problematic because emotions then drive the thought process. *If someone has got you to be emotional, then they have control over you.* They may be deliberately trying to wind you up, or get sympathy, or sell you something, or whatever, but your emotional reaction more often than not empowers others not you, unless you have good emotional control.

At these times, it can be helpful to recognize that you may not be in a position or the person to change other people's negativity and destructive habits. It's often better to walk away and let other forces create a 'learning opportunity' for those trying to hurt you.

Believing in karma, makes you calmer.

At times in my life when I could feel the anger starting to build, I learned to turn the other amygdala, a two-sided structure in the brain involved in processing emotions. If I could control my amygdala then I could also not only turn the other cheek, I could respond from a better position than mere anger. And I could focus and think far more effectively.

Turn the other amygdala.

One of the several concerning things about advertising, fake news, or emotionalism, is the ability to plant ideas and images in peoples' heads that are spurious yet powerful. As we shall see in subsequent chapters, that has been elevated to an art form and combined with technology, can be extremely harmful, let alone unethical. And now social media has allowed anyone to indulge in this manipulation. We have some influencers who have no education, subject knowledge or even rationality, poisoning people with absurd ideas that are downright harmful and destructive.

"The superior man understands what is right; the inferior man understands what will sell." -- Confucius

For example, ads for products that show quick rapid weight loss, are appealing because of the promise. However, the promise is mostly fantasy because; a) it is probably not healthy to lose weight very rapidly and more importantly; b) that weight loss is hardly ever sustained (evidence suggests that fewer than 10% of people are able to maintain significant lifestyle behavior change over the long haul).

The overall impact of such messaging is to set up false expectations that lead to failure and to completely undermine the more effective messages about how to really control one's weight. In a study conducted some years ago on constant weight fluctuation[12], the researchers concluded that one of the more damaging side-effects was on people's self-esteem as they yo-yo'ed in their weight throughout their life.

"But Doc," I hear you say, "what about Free Speech?"

Okay, but what about Free Hearing?

---

[12] Brownell, K & Rodin, J (1994). Medical, Metabolic, and Psychological Effects of Weight Cycling. Arch Intern Med. 1994;154(12):1325-1330. 4

The problem is that under the cover of 'free speech' people spew out hate, misinformation, slander, all of which are potentially damaging to individuals and society as a whole.

"Well bro, you don't have to listen to it," I can hear some say.

"But you're poisoning the river."

"You don't have to swim in it, bro."

But you're still poisoning the river.

"Again, you don't have to drink it, bro."

"You're poisoning the environment and you're poisoning someone. You're assuming that everyone can accurately evaluate your poison, but the reality is they can't and you're deliberately manipulating them and harming them. You're effectively brainwashing people."

And on and on we go.

The fact is that with social media and the many channels of communication, some dangerous and totally unfounded nonsense is out there, poisoning the environment. Some of it may be deliberately being spread by hostile forces.

It seems like we overvalue the right to *say* what you want, without considering the impact it has on people who *hear* it.

The notion that we are all individuals capable of deciding our choices for ourselves, acting rationally in our best interests devoid of any outside influence is *abject nonsense*. Of course, our culture and other people are a major influence on our thinking process. Why do firms spend billions of dollars a year on advertising if that weren't the case?

However, if you accept that all of us are potentially influenced by the many aspects of the social environment, you have to make some tough choices on how to legislate for that. It's perhaps easier, and certainly more lucrative and advantageous for the powers that be, to assume that everyone is a rational individual with the ability to decide for themselves the validity of everything they see, read and hear, even if that is ostensibly a false assumption.

It is noted that countries other than the USA have much more stringent advertising standards, which, for example, prohibit any claims that don't have appropriate validation. For example, a company can't say that it is the "best" without appropriate verifiable evidence. Other countries have "truth in advertising" standards.

It's almost as if we have a rational standard that we expect ourselves and everyone else to adhere to, independent of how our brains have been trained. And as mentioned in the Introduction, it's not so much the application of logic that's the problem, it's the automatic creation and often uncritical acceptance of assumptions, which then turn into beliefs fueled by emotions, that are the main issues.

Autopilot Existence

If we train our brains by reinforcing and having the same emotional responses, then those emotional responses will shape our narratives, and these then will become self-fulfilling processes. They will be the lens through which we view the world; the structure that creates our reality. Our consciousness will be trained to support this reality. However, it is only one 'reality,' not the many possibilities of reality. That habitual narrative is rife with biases and attentional blindness.

The book *In God's Waiting Room*, is the true story of Barbara Morello-O'Donnell who had a major physical and spiritual transformation while in a coma. I believe that that transformation was more likely to happen in a coma, where many of the usual conscious mechanisms that reinforce the habitual narrative were turned off, thus making transformation more likely.

Understanding the habitual and automatic nature of our realities and narratives is the first step towards change. Then - the hard part - actually being open to different perspectives, and then the really hard part, striving for them.

This is why change happens when crises hit. The crises make it more likely that one will reconsider, if not abandon altogether, the habitual narratives. A total change of environment might also encourage change, as might a new relationship. One of the problems with a relationship is that when two people meet, they are likely to be attracted by their perspective narratives. But if one person changes their perception of reality then the relationship itself will change.

But outside major life changes and crises, how do we get a handle on different possibilities, how do we step outside our usual perceptions, how do we create a different narrative?

The key, I believe, is to learn to manage one's consciousness.

If you have trained your consciousness to keep you on script, it will make sure that you focus, see and behave through the lens of your habitual narrative. You need to turn that editor off if you want to see the possibilities beyond your blinkered perception of your self and the world.

But how?

In short, the answer is mindfulness practices. There are many meditative techniques, but they all come down to attempting to achieve one thing: turn off the conscious script editor and just experience the world, thus making the possibilities of new narratives more likely.

Medications rather than meditations are commonly used to help people cope with distressing narratives, especially anxiety and depression. However, what they seem to do when they are effective, is to reduce the emotion so the same narratives *are more easily tolerated*. Unless that medication relief, where it occurs, is also accompanied with a change of narrative, then it might have achieved a better physical tolerance, but it hasn't achieved the necessary change. Moreover, the medications themselves might help reinforce the narrative: that I'm a helpless person who needs chemical relief.

The emotions are the energy that drive the system and when that is reduced, while the narratives might be the same intellectually, they have lost some of their power.

As a result of emotions rule over us, we try wherever possible to minimize emotional discomfort. This leads to what Freud called "defense mechanisms" designed to protect us from significant distress, which is not adaptive. There are numerous classifications of defenses, but I like the one presented by George Valliant, a brilliant Harvard professor whom I had the privilege of meeting early in my career.

Valliant divided defense mechanisms into four categories, based on their adaptiveness. You'll see that these defenses are often used in combination with each other to magnify the effect of completely avoiding the issue. And this only conspires to keep us trapped in the same narratives, and moreover these defenses often come with strong emotion, which only conspire to ingrain the narratives even more.

The fact is that these defenses don't just happen when we have to confront a mess, by programming the brain they are influencing the entire thought process. Here, we run into the word problem again. Because they are called "defenses" we think of them only as devices used when we're under attack. They are far more ubiquitous and important than that.

Interestingly, many of the adaptive 'defenses' reflect a mindset and behaviors that have been espoused by sages across the centuries of mankind's existence, like Jesus, Buddha and Confucius. They are not just useful in times of crisis or emotional challenge, they are foundations of character, behaviors that train your brain to be a more effective and loving human being.

Questions
1. How do you label your feelings?
2. Once you label them, what do you do about them?
3. What influences can change your perception of feelings?
4. Can you manage your emotions? How?

Chapter Nine

Defense Mechanisms

The characteristic ways of dealing with uncomfortable emotions involve creating more acceptable narratives about them. This leads to the concept of defense mechanisms and ultimately cognitive bias. It's about how we deal with emotional conflict.

This is an important part of consciousness and "thinking". If our emotions drive perception and thinking, how we manage particularly uncomfortable emotions will drive our thought processes, leading to more neuro-construction, i.e. training the brain.

Understanding the ways we respond to emotional states, is therefore critical in understanding our thought process.

Psychotic defenses involve different types of denial, from disbelief, to abdication of responsibility to physical conversion symptoms where the unconscious conflicts manifest as physical problems.

Let's use a simple example to see how these defenses are used.

Let's assume that a couple have been shopping and that the husband has been loudly sarcastic to his wife in the earshot of others at the store. She suggested that they buy some ice-cream and he sarcastically said, "Like that is really going to keep us healthy," and stomped off.

Denial:

Wife: "You were really mean to me in the store."

Husband: "You're kidding me, right? I didn't do anything."

Projection

Wife: "You were really mean to me in the store."

Husband: "No, it was you who were mean to me. You embarrassed me in the store by asking me that!"

Fantasy

Wife: "You were really mean to me in the store."

Husband: "No way, I was just defending myself. I thought you were going to throw that thing at me!"

Physical Conversion

Wife: "You were really mean to me in the store."

Husband: "I have such a headache. I think it's a migraine."

Now note that in Freudian terms, conversion meant that the person would actually feel pain or be sick. Often this can manifest as a real physical symptom. Of course, when you're sick there's also the benefit that you will get sympathy and avoid the issue, which is the whole point of the exercise, consciously or otherwise.

Splitting, or dividing the world into binary, good or bad distinctions, and often projecting them onto others.

Wife: "You were really mean to me in the store."

Husband: "I'm never mean. If anything, you are the mean one in this relationship."

As you can tell these are not effective ways of dealing with the issue, they are ways of denying your behavior and creating a narrative that not only doesn't address the issue but attacks the other person by projecting on to them even worse versions of the characteristic that you are being accused of. In other words, you overestimate yourself and underestimate others (see **Social Desirability Bias**)

Immature defenses also manifest as an inability to deal with reality and include such devices as acting out, fantasy, idealization, passive-aggression, wishful thinking and projection. These strategies are common amongst those diagnosed with various personality disorders.

Fantasy involves creating a whole new, fictional narrative that explains the reaction in more positive ways.

Wife: "You were really mean to me in the store."

Husband: "No way! I was just kidding with you. It was just a joke. Don't be so sensitive."

Idealization is a way of reframing the action in an extremely positive way.

Wife: "You were really mean to me in the store."

Husband: "Personally, I thought I showed a lot of restraint. Not many people would have been as kind as I was."

Passive-Aggressive speaks for itself. Passive behavior that is really aggressive. Often the avoidance of the topic is itself an aggressive, disrespectful gesture.

Wife: "You were really mean to me in the store."

Husband: "What are we having for dinner tonight?"

Neurotic defenses are considered common in adults and do have some short-term advantages but can cause long-term problems. It's interesting to note that rationalization is considered a neurotic defense mechanism when it seems to underpin so much of people's thinking!

Dissociation occurs when there is a disconnect between experience and emotion. This is common in traumatized patients as the mind tries to protect itself from re-experiencing painful experiences. It can do that, because the different aspects of memory, including the emotion of the experience, are housed in different areas of the brain. As a result, some of the aspects of an experience might not be remembered consciously. It is why trauma patients sometimes recount horrific experiences without any noticeable sign of emotion.

Wife: "You were really mean to me in the store."

Husband: "What are you talking about? I don't remember that."

Wife: "You know, when I asked whether we should get some ice cream and you stomped off."

Husband: "I don't recall stomping off, or anything like that. I just said it would be better if we didn't have it."

Rationalization is a common defense in that it doesn't really address the behavior but reframes it as totally 'logical.'

Wife: "You were really mean to me in the store."

Husband: "No, I wasn't. Don't you recall we had agreed to keep sweets and deserts out of the house? I was just affirming what we had both decided."

Regression is the use of a response that belongs in a much less mature state of development, typically, a regression into a childish behavior.

Wife: "You were really mean to me in the store."

Husband (in child-like voice): "Yes, mommy I'll try to be better next time. But you told me I couldn't have ice cream."

Repression might be better described as suppression when we totally forget what happened.

Wife: "You were really mean to me in the store."

Husband: "I have no idea what you're talking about? Do you feel OK?"

At this point most female readers and many male readers will consider this guy a total jerk. But let's give him a chance to get it right. And let's also reflect on our own behavior. Have you ever used any of the defenses above? If your answer is 'No' please go into time-out and think about your past conflicts. And then read the next section.

Mature defenses deal with the emotional issues at hand and integrate the desire to be emotionally comfortable with rational thought and self-awareness. Moreover, they do something else that is critical. They are not intended to defend the ego to the point of narcissism, but they are *prepared to accept responsibility and consider the other person's feelings and perceptions.*

As you shall see in the next chapter, Mature defense include amongst others; acceptance, courage, emotional self-regulation, forgiveness, gratitude, humility, humor, mindfulness, patience and respect.

So, let's give the guy a chance to get it right.

Acceptance is owning up to your behavior. It often requires courage and is the platform for forgiveness. It's saying Yes to your mess.

Wife: "You were really mean to me in the store."

Husband: "Yes, I was. I'm sorry if I embarrassed you."

Emotional self-regulation is the ability to manage your emotions and not be dependent on other's views for emotional comfort.

Wife: "You were really mean to me in the store."

Husband: "Yes, that was really an over-reaction. I don't know what came over me. If you see me doing that again will you please point it out to me?"

Gratitude and *respect* are also expressions of humility.

Wife: "You were really mean to me in the store."

Husband: "I'm so sorry. I love you and am so grateful that we're together. I never want to be mean like that to you, of all people."

And a little dash of *humor* can help, along with the humility.

Wife: "You were really mean to me in the store."

Husband: "I'm so sorry. I was such a jerk. And what's worse, that's my favorite ice-cream!!"

Mature defenses would definitely include the willingness to look at one's thinking and narrative and be prepared to change it based on objective analysis of the facts and other perspectives. I will go into these in more detail in the next chapter.

Questions
  1. What defense mechanisms do you use?
  2. What are examples of mature defenses that you have used?
  3. How could you learn to use mature defenses more often?

Chapter Ten

Morality and Wisdom

The mature defenses are considered effective ways of adapting to life's travails. These behaviors underpin the ideal mindset, the one that will be the most effective in adapting to life. And these are states of mind and being *that will train your brain to be more balanced in your emotions and thoughts.* In many ways, they are antidotes to all sorts of bias, including the biases inherent in our thinking.

There is a connection between the heart and the brain, and these 'defenses' represent the influence of the heart, which is a key player in the autonomic nervous system that manages out emotional states.

And the key is to manage emotional states. Emotions are signals that we need to pay attention to, but then manage and put in to perspective. We can't let our emotions dictate our behavior. We can let our *considered thoughts* about a situation, that has been made noticeable by our emotions, drive our actions.

Inevitably, these defenses focus on situations that give rise to emotions, and that is why they are so important – they show the effective ways of adapting to situations and thus training our thought processes, too.

These defenses are also behaviors that have been defined as moral guides in that they place responsibility within each of us to accept our condition and adapt in a way that doesn't harm us, but elevates us, doesn't harm others but potentially elevates them, too.

Acceptance:
"Acceptance of what has happened is the first step to overcoming the consequences of any misfortune." – William James

The root of any adaptation is to accept your situation. Remember, acceptance doesn't mean agreement, but it is a platform for your future path and goals.

It's very easy and maybe even natural to stay rooted in your anger in the unfairness of it all; or the seeming unfairness of it all (see the **Just World** bias). And they surely are cases where that would be completely justified, for example, when someone has been imprisoned for years for a crime they didn't commit. However, most of us have consequences that we contributed to in some way or another. Sure, the punishment may have been excessive or even unwarranted, but you cannot dwell on it.

Moreover, anger and resentment simply *reinforcs the mind to feel and see victimization everywhere*. It may indeed be there, but that's not the point. The goal is your recovery, and your effective adaptation. There are times when it might be useful for you to use anger to motivate you to do what you need to do for your adaptation and development. However, the anger is not a goal in itself and neither should it dictate your actions.

If you do not accept the reality of where you are, you will always be trapped in it.

As we have seen, the perception of context is critical to thoughts, feelings and behaviors. Viktor Frankl, a holocaust survivor, made this critical point in his book *Man's Search for Meaning*; that as soon as a situation (even a concentration camp) has meaning, the suffering disappears or at least is severely minimized. Frankl helped give psychological and medical advice to his fellow inmates, turning a hell, into a context where help has incredible purpose and meaning.

Having a realistic understanding of any situation is a team effort, that might involve many people. It is very easy, indeed the norm, to deceive ourselves and we need other perspectives not just to have an accurate understanding of any situation but also how to adapt to it.

Questions
1. What are the situations that are currently bothering you?
2. How do you know you have an accurate perception of those situations?
3. Have you accepted the reality of these situations?
4. If not, why not?
5. How has your acceptance or lack of acceptance influenced your thoughts about yourself, others and life in general?

Altruism:
Every man must decide whether he will walk in the light of creative altruism or in the darkness of destructive selfishness. -- Martin Luther King, Jr.

The essence of existence is interdependence and compassion. It is where happiness comes from (see below). The road to helping yourself and discovering your worth has to include helping others.

Helping others not only gives you a sense of purpose but it also helps put your own issues into perspective. Service also helps you do something very critical – it helps you get outside of your own ego, which is important in all of these healthy ways of coping, and is the key to a spiritual life.

Even the seemingly small acts of kindness you do for others, can have amazing benefits.

Questions
1. What service and volunteering activities have you done in the past? How meaningful were they to you?
2. What altruistic activities do you currently engage in?

3. What altruistic activities are available to you?
4. What altruistic opportunities would be the most meaningful to you now?
5. When and how are you going to pursue new volunteering and service opportunities?

Anticipation:

Perfect Planning Prevents Pathetic Persecution

One of the key reasons to accept and be realistic about your situation is that, by doing so, you can anticipate and prepare from any potential fall-out from it. This applies to both your and other people's future reactions.

If you know you are going into a potentially stressful situation, how will you plan to handle it? More stress will mean less rationality, which could set you up for even more criticism and stress.

This could also apply to supposedly "positive" future events. If you won the lottery, how would that change you, if at all? Would it change your values and your thinking? There have been some very sad and scary stories about lottery winners, that include suicide and murder. Which is why I am seriously thinking about taking out insurance in case I win the lottery.

A we shall see, *temporal discounting*, the tendency to undervalue the future, is a major cognitive bias that prevents many people from planning effectively about anything, let alone their emotional states.

Questions
1. Do you ever anticipate future emotional states?
2. How have you responded (or do you think you would respond) if others attack you?

3. What is your most effective strategy when being confronted with different views and interpretations?
4. How can you prepare an effective response for those who attack you?
5. Who can help you devise and implement and effective strategy against attacks?

Compassion:
"The purpose of human life is to serve, and to show compassion and the will to help others." –Albert Schweitzer

The essence of morality is how we treat others. And our meaning and purpose is also revealed by how we treat others. And so is our happiness.

Being compassionate, therefore, is an essential skill both for acting and thinking. Compassion is central to adaptation. It is key to forgiveness and several other of the mature defenses. It involves respect and humility.

Compassion for others doesn't mean agreement or tolerance. It simply recognizes that they are human beings subject to the same forces as you. That they are human beings who also want control but may have implemented an inappropriate way of finding it.

Compassion is also a reminder that you don't know.

You don't know the circumstances surrounding someone's behavior and opinion.

You don't know what experiences they have had that led them to their views, emotions and behavior.

You don't know how you would think and act if you were exposed to exactly the same life circumstances as that person.

Compassion is, therefore, the default recognition of our ignorance, and our wisdom.

There was a priest who was interviewing captured German soldiers during World War II. He asked one of them whether he was sorry that he had killed people.

The soldier said that he was not sorry that he had killed.

Then the priest asked him a more profound question.

"Are you sorry that you're not sorry?"

I remember an experience as a young child. We were living in North London and my grandmother had just moved in with us. She would occasionally take me to the movies. One time, when I was about four or five, I recall sitting through a movie and at its typical emotional ending, I found myself crying. I couldn't understand it. Why was I crying? I mean crying was associated with pain and I wasn't hurt. I had found the outward expression of compassion.

There can be some confusion about how compassion manifests. It's one thing to understand how someone is feeling but what you do about is another matter entirely. Sometimes, unbridled compassion can be mistakenly transformed into codependency.

"We should feel sorrow but not sink under its oppression." -
Confucius

Questions
1. Do you consider yourself compassionate?
2. What have the consequences been of your compassion?
3. How have you experienced other people's compassion?
4. Do you think most of your friends are compassionate?
5. What influences in your life encourage compassion? Discourage compassion?

Courage:

"Mistakes are always forgivable, if one has the courage to admit them." -- Bruce Lee

As you can tell, you need courage to face up authentically to life. You need courage to deal with the painful emotions that accompany confronting your difficulties and mistakes. And you need courage to deal with situations that are problematic for you.

However, the key here is what is your perception of courage? Is it courage to face the hurricane of helplessness, stress or even the invective, hypocrisy and hate of others? If so, you might be completely terrified and overwhelmed.

On the other hand, if your perception of courage is about you, and not others, about digging down and treating yourself with respect, of fighting off the evil forces within you, then you'll see that immense courage is not only very possible but entirely liberating.

And when you act courageously, you'll soon find that you have moved to a position where courage is no longer necessary because there's nothing to be afraid of that you can't handle.

I was writing down quotes for this book. Some I was creating and some came from others, and they are attributed throughout the book. When I looked at the quotes the following day, I came across this one. I have looked all over to see whether it was created by someone else, but can't find it. So, let's all share it.

"Once you go courageously into battle with others you're battle hardened. Once you go courageously into battle aligned with yourself, it's not a battle any more."

Questions:
1. What situations in life scare you?
2. How can you/have you displayed courage in dealing with

difficult situations in the past?

3. How can you summon up the courage to deal with your conflicts?

4. Who can help you be courageous?

5. What do you need to be courageous? (No, it's not alcohol).

Emotional Regulation:

"If your emotional abilities aren't in hand, if you don't have self-awareness, if you are not able to manage your distressing emotions, if you can't have empathy and have effective relationships, then no matter how smart you are, you are not going to get very far." -- Daniel Goleman

Managing your emotions is the key to success in any endeavor. As we have seen, thoughts and emotions are incredibly interlinked. If your emotions are out of control, so is everything about you, from your actions to your health. It's possible, if not likely, that poor emotional regulation led you to your worst decisions and actions. In which case, controlling emotions is important so you don't repeat the same destructive behaviors.

In addition, controlling feelings of anger, guilt, shame, frustration and depression are important in giving you the focus and energy you need to deal with your situation in an adaptive light. This is about adaptation, not necessarily about feeling positive. I'm not asking you to smile and blow it off, although as you'll see later in this chapter, humor definitely has its place.

I get concerned that the positive psychology movement is misunderstood as just putting a smile on your face and everything will be just fine. I actually prefer the term *adaptive psychology* because it avoids the possible misconception that being happy is the same as success. To reiterate an earlier point, success is about adaptation, not pleasure. And as we shall see there is a popular misconception about happiness.

The best way of learning to control emotions is through mindfulness and meditation practice and some of these exercises are described later. When you develop some control of your consciousness, you'll be able to distance yourself from your emotions. You can see them as signals and analyze them, rather than being completely overrun by them.

Questions
1.   Which emotions do you find the most difficult to deal with?
2.   How do you currently deal with uncomfortable feelings?
3.   How could you manage your emotions more effectively?
4.   What can you do today to start better emotion management?
5.   How can others help you improve your emotion management?

Emotional Self-Sufficiency:
> *"The greatest thing in the world is to know how to belong to oneself." — Michel de Montaigne*

When you have developed emotional control you're going to have much better emotional self-sufficiency, which means you will not be unduly influenced by other people's emotions. And in today's world, there's no shortage of people wanting to intimidate you, if not shame you, by venting their emotions.

The best response to such a situation is, of course, not to react to other people's emotional outbursts. That's their problem, don't make it yours.

In many of these situations, these people are merely projecting their own issues onto you, so don't accept them. In fact, don't even open the envelope, *return to sender*.

If you respond from a position of control, rather than react from a position of impulse, you win. Remember, respond not react.

Don't be nasty to them. You can smile, politely. You don't even have to say anything. Sometimes, silence is golden.

Questions
1.   Are you easily intimidated by others, who bring up your indiscretions in an emotional, accusatory way?
2.   How do you typically act when someone attacks you based on your past mistakes?
3.   If this has happened in the past how did you react?
4.   How could you respond?
5.   What do you need to do to establish emotional self-sufficiency.

Forgiveness:
"To forgive is to set a prisoner free and discover that the prisoner was you." -- Lewis B. Smedes

Let's get this straight, forgiveness is not a free pass. However, forgiveness of self and others is very important, for two critical reasons.

Forgiveness is letting go of the anger you have towards someone else or yourself. And as we saw in the section on Acceptance, letting go of that anger is critical for you, not just or even for the person who you believe has wronged you. It is a key part of acceptance.

The other important aspect is that forgiveness does not necessarily imply lack of consequences for an action. It might be, for example, that a victim asks for a written apology from a perpetrator rather than suing them. Punishment is relative, so it can be scaled.

Forgiveness is also a chance to do better next time.

It also turns out that severe punishment might not actually be corrective. It would be mistaken to assume that dire consequences always act as a deterrent; certainly not for everybody. It is one of the problems and biases that affect the prison system. If you treat people like criminals why would you expect them to be any different?

Remember the cognitive bias of *temporal discounting*? We live in the present and a future deterrent might not be sufficient incentive to curb an inappropriate behavior. Moreover, a dire punishment might also lead to anger and revenge that are more likely to lead to further criminal activity.

With forgiveness, you are leading by example, a very dignified example. Maybe others will appreciate it and learn from it.

And here's two critical lines form the Lord's Prayer that can be misunderstood:

"Forgive us our trespasses, as we forgive those who trespass against us."

What that means is, "Please forgive me, *because* I forgive others."

Asking for forgiveness when you don't practice it yourself would be hypocritical.

Indeed, the challenge of successful adaptation characterized by these mature defenses, is that you make the commitment to pursue them regardless of whether others practice them or not. One of the keys to adaptation (and redemption) is that you stop judging others and focus on your own behavior. It is very easy to get sidetracked and deflected from the path to wisdom by looking at others rather than yourself.

For example, someone might criticize you for your beliefs, past indiscretions or other behavior and you respond with an attack of your own against them.

"I'll give him a taste of his own medicine," you say to yourself with some bravado.

The problem is that you don't want to give him a taste of his medicine, you want to give him a *taste of your medicine.*

His medicine – judgment and attack – is toxic and exchanging it will do nothing except poison you both. Your *medicine is based in adaptation, wisdom and virtue*, recognizing your indiscretions and using them as impetus for major change in your life.

When you don't rise to the bait of hate, you demonstrate you have more control than the baiter. As it says in the bible:

"But to you who are listening I say: Love your enemies, do good to those who hate you, bless those who curse you, pray for those who mistreat you. If someone slaps you on one cheek, turn to them the other also. If someone takes your coat, do not withhold your shirt from them. Give to everyone who asks you, and if anyone takes what belongs to you, do not demand it back. Do to others as you would have them do to you." (Luke 6:27-31)

Or as Oscar Wilde put it:
"Always forgive your enemies – nothing annoys them so much."

Questions
1. Have you ever forgiven yourself?
2. Have you ever forgiven others?
3. Have you ever carried a grudge for a long time?
4. If so, what were the effects of the grudge?
5. How did it feel when you forgave others? What were the consequences?

Gratitude:
"Gratitude makes sense of our past, brings peace for today, and creates a vision for tomorrow." -- Melody Beattie

Perspective makes all the difference in the mental process. It determines where you focus and where you concentrate. (Focus is where you put your attention, concentration is how deeply you do it.) As mentioned elsewhere in this book, we live in the present and therefore tend to focus on what is happening right this moment, which is often unimportant and inconsequential compared to other aspects of life. One of the problems of living in the here and now is that it is very easy, actually the default position, to judge events and have a perspective that is short-term rather than a bigger, overarching perspective.

For example, it is easier to yell back in anger at a hater, rather than keep a broader perspective that his or her anger really have nothing to do with you. (see **Reactance Bias**)

Do you know how lucky you are to actually exist? If you consider all the natural biological and chemical processes that have to align to give life, simple existence is a miracle. Then consider the near misses that you have had that could have killed or disabled you.

When I was in elementary school, one day I was the first kid to rush out to recess. I remember rushing out to the playground but slipped just before I emerged from the covered entryway. Which was good because at the same time a truck was barreling into the yard and would have surely hit me head on if I hadn't slipped.

Then, a couple of years ago, my old Camry had to go into the shop and I had a rental car, a small SUV, for a couple of days. On the second day, a car crossed over into my lane and hit me head on. I broke my sternum and was concussed but I might not be around to write this book if I had been in my old Camry.

Sure, it is easy to get frustrated and get stressed when things don't go well. However, we cannot take life for granted. It's a miracle and we need to continually see the big picture and count our blessings.

When you're having a tough day at work, do you ever stop to consider that today, several people were told of their terminal illness diagnosis? Do you ever stop to consider that in Syria or Afghanistan, someone has just seen their entire family blown up? Do you ever consider that today in various countries, numerous young children died of malnutrition?

We need to stop more often and appreciate the miracle of life. When my dog, an English Setter named Jack, looks me directly in the eye and we are literally sharing the moment, I am blown away.

And how about some of these facts:
• Nerve impulses sent from the brain move at a speed of 274 km/h.

• A single human brain generates more electrical impulses in a day than all the telephones of the world combined.

• The human heart pumps 182 million liters of blood during the average lifetime.

• 50,000 cells in your body died and were replaced by new ones while you were reading this sentence

You can find out more about the miracle of your body at https://brightside.me/article/100-quick-and-fascinating-facts-about-the-human-body-38305/

You can appreciate the miracle of your life by reminding yourself every day about your blessings.

Questions
1. Are you mindful of how lucky you are?
2. What are you grateful for?
3. How can you stay more mindful and grateful of your blessings?
4. Do you relate the events in your life to a higher purpose?
5. Do you have family and friends who practice gratitude?

Honesty

"Honesty is the fastest way to prevent a mistake from turning into a failure." – James Altucher

Honesty is sometimes not mentioned as an adaptive defense mechanism. Honesty is part of acceptance, and refers as much about honesty with yourself as with others. However, sometimes the facts can be unclear, and the situation vague. How do you act then?

There was a situation in my life that I second-guessed for many years and it concerned this very topic.

My dad was a good guy, with a nice sense of humor and an unbelievable acumen for mental arithmetic. He had very little education, and if he had somehow acquired some, he would probably have been a mathematician or physicist, rather than a bookie. However, he was also incredibly stressed and sometimes had a hard time coping with mundane matters, let alone important ones.

In my mid-twenties, while I was embarking on my psychology career, he got colon cancer and required a colostomy. Being the "doctor" in the family, I was deputed by my mother and sister to liaise with the treating medical team and report back to them the latest news and opinion.

A few months after his first procedure, my dad underwent surgery again. Following the procedure, I spoke with the surgical team. They had reversed the colostomy. Great! However, the reason they had done so was that the cancer had spread and there was no more that could be done for him. He had an estimated year to live.

My immediate thought was, "How is he ever going to deal with his impending death. He can't change a light bulb without getting frustrated."

I spoke with the doctors about it, and they agreed that telling him outright may be more than he could take. I suggested that perhaps that I could imply he was living on borrowed time without actually telling him he had a few months to live. I hatched the plan.

I told my dad, my mother and my sister that the surgery had gone okay BUT there was always a chance that the cancer could return. So, we should all be grateful for every day and treasure it because no one knows how long he actually might have.

I didn't tell my sister or my mother any more than that because I didn't want to put them in an impossibly difficult situation.

My dad enjoyed a good few months. He and my mother went on a couple of vacations and visited friends and relatives. My sister and I made concerted efforts to spend time with him. Then he died at the age of 61.

I have always second-guessed myself on my decision. When I subsequently told my mother and sister what I knew but hadn't told them, there were not angry, just very accepting.

Had I been dishonest?

You decide.

More recently, having studied and researched medical

communication, I realized that statistics can be misleading (see the section on cognitive bias in healthcare). There are examples of people who are told that they have only a few months to live and survive decades. Medical opinion is based on group statistics and the prognosis might not apply to any one individual. However, I wasn't aware of that at the time and don't recall it being part of my thinking.

The key here is honesty with yourself. Are you honestly accepting a situation? Are you specifically being honest about your motives and actions? Then, given what you know, are you honestly conveying that with others? And perhaps most of all, is that honesty driven by love and respect, of yourself and others?

We have already considered temporal discounting, the tendency to live in the present. That might lead you to be dishonest to protect yourself right now. However, that dishonesty is likely to rebound on you in the future. As a result, I think it is useful to embrace the notion, that anything you do will be eventually revealed.

There will be no secrets.

"Fear is the natural reaction of moving closer to the truth." -- *Pema Chodron*

Questions
1.   Do you consider yourself an honest person?
2.   Have you ever lied?
3.   What have the consequences been of any lies you have told?
4.   Have you ever been lied to? How did it feel?
5.   How can you become more honest with yourself and others?

Humility:
"Humility is not thinking less of yourself, it's thinking of yourself less." -- *Rick Warren*

It takes both competition and cooperation for adaptive evolution. In the western, capitalist tradition, the focus is on competition, which can frame your narrative in terms of strength, winning and success. However, life is about balance and you also need to be an interdependent cooperator as well as an independent competitor. Bravado has its place but so does humility.

The wise person really acknowledges what he doesn't know. He or she acknowledges that one never knows the whole story about anything and that, for the most part, the human mind works on bias not objective evidence. Recognizing what you don't know isn't ignorance, it's the height of wisdom. Recognizing that you are always a work in progress, isn't negative self-talk but an adaptive reality of life.

Humble pie doesn't make you gain weight. It's good for you. It's a really adaptive tactic that will help you not overestimate your talents, and thus set you up for successful adaptation.

"For everyone who exalts himself will be humbled, and everyone who humbles himself will be exalted." – Jesus Christ

Questions
1. Do you maintain a humble perspective about yourself?
2. Are there times when you can be arrogant?
3. What are the circumstances associated with being less than humble?
4. Are you aware trying to maintain a humble perspective?
5. What can you do to reinforce humility?

Humor:
"Comedy is simply a funny way of being serious." -- Peter Ustinov

Humor is an interesting defense. It allows for the airing or discussion of hurts, while at the same time applying the anesthetic. It's a bit like deliberately hurting yourself as you knock back the painkillers. Physiologically, laughter is a medicine.

One of my favorite stories concerns Norman Cousins, a famous journalist and activist in the mid-twentieth century. In 1964 he was diagnosed with a devastating connective tissue disease and was given very little chance of recovery. In addition to moving out of the hospital and into a hotel room and taking massive doses of Vitamin C, Cousins also rented a projector and watched hours of comic movies.

Cousins later said that, "I made the joyous discovery that ten minutes of genuine belly laughter had an anesthetic effect and would give me at least two hours of pain-free sleep," and "when the pain-killing effect of the laughter wore off, we would switch on the motion picture projector again and not infrequently, it would lead to another pain-free interval." His journey was recorded in his 1979 book *Anatomy of an Illness.*

Humor, therefore, is a way of addressing pain, in different forms, while at the same time producing endorphins. Some of the best humor is about human frailties, and the sorts of topics we would want to shy away from if they weren't put in the context of laughter.

Moreover, making fun of yourself isn't likely to offend anyone and allows you to present yourself as understanding, accepting of responsibility, while at the same time getting a sympathetic response from your audience. It helps in the re-perception of you.

Seeing the humor in things, especially your own behavior, is a way of associating thinking about your transgressions with positive feelings.

Now we don't want to go overboard and force it. I am not suggesting your force yourself into feeling upbeat when you're not feeling it. One of the problems with positive psychology is the notion that it is all about feeling good, it isn't. Remember this is about adaptation, not fun.

"When you first get up in the morning smile, and get it over with."
-- W.C. Fields

Questions:
1. Have you ever heard someone tell about their indiscretions with humor?
2. How did you respond?
3. Can you retell your story with humor?
4. How often do you watch amusing movies, programs and other comedic material?
5. How many of your friends and family have a good sense of humor?

Mercy:
"Blessed are the merciful, for they will be shown mercy." – Jesus Christ

The Merriam Webster dictionary defines mercy as "compassion or forbearance shown especially to an offender or to one subject to one's power" and "a blessing that is an act of divine favor or compassion."

In many ways, mercy is the height of emotional control. At precisely the moment when you might feel the right to be angry and vengeful, you instead show emotional control by being merciful. You are not controlled by the habitual parameters of the mind but transcend them, showing your real power, strength and wisdom.

There are many situations where you can be merciful. And for those of us who have asked for mercy for our own transgressions, being merciful seems an important characteristic, unless you want to be a hypocrite.

This again, comes from being a person with values; that we won't ask from others what we couldn't or wouldn't give to them.

Questions
1. Has anyone ever showed you mercy? If so, how did you feel?
2. Have you ever showed someone mercy? If so, how did you feel?
3. What are the consequences of showing mercy?
4. Can you think of a current situation where you could be more merciful?
5. Do you have merciful friends and family?

Mindfulness:
"Mindfulness is a way of befriending ourselves and our experience." – Jon Kabat-Zinn

Mindfulness has become something of a buzz word recently and for good reason. Although the word is used to mean anything from meditation to awareness, at its core mindfulness is increasingly an essential life skill for several reasons.

In our busy, stressful lives, when there is so much competing for our attention, it is easy to go through life simply checking off the To Do list. It is easy to focus on the actions we have to take, not on their meaning and purpose. It is easy to be completely distracted. Mindfulness helps us appreciate and better understand what maybe our greatest gift, our consciousness.

Mindfulness is about learning how to look at what is going on in your mind and separate yourself from it. You can become an observer of your mind, rather than habitually and mindlessly getting caught up in the machinations and habits that you have programmed in it. In today's world, there are so many distractions that we can end up rubbernecking our way through life, paying attention to irrelevant and meaningless things which potentially sucks the joy and meaning out of us.

Mindfulness is about looking at your thoughts and emotions, which gives you a better chance of not just understanding them but managing them.

Mindfulness practices include a variety of techniques that calm you down as well as give you some objectivity about what is passing through your mind. There's a lot of research into Mindfulness Based Stress Reduction (MBSR) techniques, pioneered by Jon Kabat-Zinn, that show that they can improve mood and anxiety, as well as stress and pain.

Mindfulness trains your focus and attention so you can look without distraction at the important areas of your life, including the inside of your mind. The ability to calm your mind and not get caught up in the chaos of your emotions also facilitates two other important skills.

The first is the ability to be in the moment and appreciate it; to experience rather than to analyze. This is a critical mindset that underpins several of the adaptive defenses, like gratitude, humility, respect, etc.

Managing your consciousness and emotions also allows you to clarify your thoughts and be more rational as well as creative. When running high, emotions drive the narrative and can lead to all sorts of unhealthy beliefs about yourself and others, and as a result, lead to poor decision-making.

Questions:
1. Have you ever practiced a form of mindfulness?
2. Do you ever stop to analyze the thoughts in your head, or do you just accept them?
3. Do you ever stop your mind, from processing and try to switch off?
4. Do you know any people who practice mindfulness or

meditation?
5.   How do you unwind?

Moderation:

"A wise man is superior to any insults which can be put upon him, and the best reply to unseemly behavior is patience and moderation." -- Moliere.

Moderation is almost a dirty word in today's culture. It's often represented as a sign of apathy or weakness, or fence-sitting rather than wisdom and balance. That's exactly what one would expect from a culture based on emotionalism and sensationalism. Except that it creates a major problem.

Because thought is influenced by emotions, the more emotional one is, the more "committed" you seem to be. Can you be passionately middle-of-the-road? Can you be ecstatic about wisdom when it is focused on reminders of what you don't know???

What emotionalism leads to is extremism, the reign of emotions and the demise of rationality. Sound familiar?

Moreover, in a world that treasures and glorifies success at almost any cost, moderation can sound weak, like you're not trying hard enough, or a wimp or even a sell-out.

Rather than being a sign of weakness or a wimp, moderation is a sign of wisdom. It is a sign of someone in control of their emotions (see Mindfulness above)

"The meek shall inherit the earth…"

The meek here are not the wimps and fence-sitters but those with emotional control and wisdom. They will inherit the earth because all the emotional extremists will have neutralized each other

…hopefully.

Moderation is therefore an important skill to develop…in everything.

It's easy to be moderate on issues and behaviors that have little interest to you. That's not moderation, just disinterest. The real trick is to be moderate on the things you're passionate about.

Moderation is the brake in your race car – the race car named Desire.

Moderation may sound like a dopamine buster, but it isn't. I'm not saying you shouldn't have a good time, but perhaps I'm suggesting we redefine what a "good time" is. Happiness isn't about pleasure, it's about meaning, virtue and satisfaction.

Studies in happiness around the world show that it is not about pleasure, but more about meaning, purpose and virtue. Pleasure is fleeting and cannot be sustained. Or if it could be, there would be serious problems. Have you ever heard of happy protesters? You would have to constantly believe that everything was perfect, an awful state to be in.

In materialist societies, ownership seems the path to happiness, but it isn't. In fact, studies show that over about the equivalent of $70,000 per year in the U.S., money adds little to happiness. Not surprisingly, the biggest contributor to happiness is a purposeful life and the biggest detractors, anxiety and depression.

Ironically then, in dealing with stressors or even your mistakes, the redemptive journey might provide you with the greatest happiness even if it is associated with less money and fewer material things.

"Happiness is not a goal; it is a by-product." -- Eleanor Roosevelt.

Another big issue is that excess rather than moderation, changes the brain in ways you might not have considered.

Cocaine can increase the amount of dopamine released by up to 10x, compared to sex, which might increase it by 2x. So, now you artificially give yourself a brief but mind-blowing sense of pleasure. As a result, the appeal of everything else and natural pleasures, like sex and food, for example, are reduced by comparison. Consequently, the mind-blowing pleasure reduces normal experience to a depressed and deprived state, leading to depression and addiction.

Practice moderation in all things. The moderate person is the strong person.

"Total abstinence is easier than perfect moderation," said St Augustine. He was talking about sex, but the comment applies to any behavior. Moderation isn't easy but it's where your sense of balance, sense of self, and wisdom come from.

Questions
1. Are you moderate in all things?
2. What areas do you have difficulty with moderation?
3. Have you successfully managed to become moderate in one of your passions?
4. What would it take for you to develop moderation?
5. What steps can you take today to improve moderation?

Patience:
"Adopt the pace of nature: her secret is patience." – Ralph Waldo Emerson

The key here is to be willing to see gradual progress. Sometimes going slowly allows events to evolve and for you to see the process from different perspectives.

If you have a goal that is really important to you, like maximizing the gift of reasoning, you will have patience. Besides, it is the height of wisdom to recognize that any worthwhile transformation is an evolving process, with no time limits or boundaries.

Moreover, it is always a good idea to copy nature. Any time you try to go against it, you are risking some seriously negative consequences.

Continuing the theme of inter-relatedness of all of these effective, mature defense mechanisms, patience goes along with moderation and mindfulness, as well as the others described herein.

Questions
1.   Are you a patient person?
2.   Can you a think of a time when your patience paid off?
3.   Can you think of a time when your impatience actually hurt you?
4.   How can you improve your patience?
5.   What can you do today to improve your patience?

Respect:
"Respect your efforts, respect yourself. Self-respect leads to self-discipline. When you have both firmly under your belt, that's real power." -- Clint Eastwood

Respect is based in non-judgment. You do not judge others, because you are in no position to do so. This is a good place to start.

You might have to relearn how to give respect. In today's emotional and judgmental culture, it is easy to give in to uninformed, unsubstantiated opinions designed to rile up your emotions. Here are some questions to ask yourself, and reminders, in these situations.

- How much do I really know about this person?

- How truthful are the things being said about them?

- Where can I find out the truth, if at all?
- Am I being manipulated?

- Until I am sure for myself, I can't believe what is said.

- If I want people to respect me, I have to respect them.

- I may not agree with this person but that doesn't mean I have the right to disrespect their right to their own views and opinions.

Part of the importance of respect is that you don't know the full story. Respect doesn't mean you endorse, agree with, condone, or tolerate.

For example, you encounter someone who has been accused of child sexual abuse. This is a sensitive topic for you because you have been there. You want to spit on him, you're so mad. You're about as far away as respecting someone as you can go. How can he possibly understand what he has done to his accuser!

However, what you don't know is that the himself was horribly abused as a child, and one way of coping with that, is to somehow justify it, that can lead some people in that situation to perpetrate the very abuse that torments them.

Oh, and the accusation turns out to be false.

You have way more in common than you think.

Unfortunately, the brain works on contrast and completely overvalues and exaggerates the differences, then reifies them, totally forgetting or ignoring the similarities. As mentioned earlier, human beings are genetically 99.5% the same. However, we can take that minor difference and make it the defining characteristic of our relationship, rather than focusing on the massive similarities.

Questions
1. Do you have a group of people that you disrespect as a whole?
2. Do you find yourself making instant judgments about people?
3. Do you ever try to challenge the instant disrespect you might feel for a person or a group by realizing it's a gross (in **both sense** of the word) generalization?
4. Are you colleagues and friends respectful?
5. Why do you respect the people that you do?

Suppression:
"We can never give up; we only exchange one thing for another"
— *Sigmund Freud*

Suppression is another mature and adaptive tactic in which you make a conscious effort to stop thinking about negative scenarios and obsessing on negative feelings and narratives.

This conscious effort will be much easier if you have practiced mindfulness and it turns out have actually made the attempt to suppress difficult memories.

An article by Heather Berlin and Chris Koch in a 2009 Scientific American article sheds some light on this.
(https://www.scientificamerican.com/article/neuroscience-meets-psychoanalysis/

They write about an experiment conducted by psychologist Michael Anderson and his colleagues

"Two dozen volunteers had to memorize 48 word pairs (for example, ordeal-roach or steam-train). Subsequently, while lying in a scanner, subjects were shown the first cue word and had to either recall the second, associated word (called the respond condition) or prevent it from entering consciousness (suppress condition). Actively suppressing the matched word while lying in the scanner had the effect of reducing recall of the word afterward (as compared with the respond condition); this result is not just simple forgetting that occurs with the passage of time."

Another finding was the..

"intriguing observation is that the brain is more active when *avoiding* recalling a memory than during recall itself. People suppress unwanted memories by *exerting willful effort* that can be tracked in the nervous system in ways only dreamed of by Freud."

This is an important step because as we have seen, the more emotional we are, the less focused and rational we can become. You have the control.

Questions
1. How good are you at managing your thoughts?
2. How do you suppress difficult emotions?
3. Have there been times when you didn't suppress difficult thoughts and feelings? What happened?
4. How could you improve your ability to suppress anger and frustration?
5. What could you do today to start the process of suppression?

Tolerance:
"In the practice of tolerance, one's enemy is the best teacher." – Dalai Lama

As I have already mentioned, one of the other mature defenses is moderation. That moderation applies to moderation of your thoughts and especially of automatic – and not so automatic – judgmental ideas. Being moderate in your thinking means being non-judgmental and tolerant -- tolerant of yourself and others.

Now tolerance is not the same as acceptance. You can be tolerant of someone else's views but that doesn't mean you have to accept them. This is related to respect. There's a difference between someone and their opinions.

It's easy to get mad at someone criticizing you for your behavior. However, in the same way that you would likely dismiss someone's criticism of you on the grounds of ignorance, the same applies to you. How well do you really know this person? Do you know all their experiences that are relevant to their perception of your situation? Sure, maybe there are projecting their own misgivings on to you, or trying to take advantage of your indiscretions, or just maybe they have had some horrific experiences that underpin their reactions? In the vast majority of cases, you just don't know. Give them the benefit of the doubt that you would hope they would give you. Remember, you want to give them *a taste of your medicine*, not theirs.

Questions
1. In what circumstances are you most tolerant?
2. Do you have a high or low frustration threshold?
3. How could you be more tolerant?
4. How could you remind and cue yourself to be more tolerant?
5. Who could support you in your quest for greater tolerance?

Work:
"There are no secrets to success. It is the result of preparation, hard work, and learning from failure." – Colin Powell

Action is the key to transformation. And the reason for that is that it is action that changes the brain.

Sitting around talking about a behavior or even considering it, is a necessary but not sufficient first step. It is action that ultimately changes the brain. And typically, the more prolonged and intense the action is, the more effect it will have on the brain.

Work isn't just being productive or indulging in change it is literally restructuring the brain. And without that restructuring, you will never change.

The coping strategies described in this section all require work. However, the pay-off is enormous.

Questions
1. How are you going to stay focused on your task of developing more adaptive, mature defenses?
2. Are you a hard worker?
3. Can you keep going when you are ready to quit?
4. What do you need to develop your persistence and perseverance?
5. Do you have good role models who demonstrate a great work ethic?

Chapter Eleven

Cognitive Bias

It is extremely difficult to accurately weigh all the factors that influence our thinking, decisions and predictions. Cognitive biases are tendencies that distort or exaggerate our attempts to arrive at a balanced view of a situation. They are often subconscious.

These various default mechanisms of the brain referenced throughout the book, lead to cognitive biases, which overly influence our thinking and behavior. This is not an exhaustive summary but some of the main forms of bias at play every day in our lives.

Anchoring refers to the notion that, for example, the first price mentioned about a product anchors expectations about it. So, in an infomercial the first price mentioned anchors expectations. This still has power even though many of us assume that the price is inflated. This is also very relevant in negotiations where each party stakes out their outer limit on the assumption that the two parties will agree to meet somewhere around the middle.

(Note: Many years ago, I was traveling in India and I needed to get new baggage to carry my possessions. I went into a bazaar in Ahmedebad and found a suitable backpack. When I asked the price, the salesperson quoted me 200 rupees. I countered with 60. The salesperson then countered with 150. I countered that with 50. The look of disorientation on the salesperson was remarkable. How can this be? He countered with 120. I countered with 40. More disbelief. He countered with 100. I left the store, or tried to. The salesperson agreed to 40. I had simply violated the anchoring bias. This is a great negotiating tactic if you don't care whether you buy the product or not. You don't have to split the difference.)

Confirmation Bias

This is a key bias. What it means is that we have the tendency to seek information that supports our view and dismiss information that disputes it. This allows anyone to hold fast to their views even in the face of sometimes overwhelming evidence to the contrary. It's why there is the old adage about avoiding conversation about religion or politics. It's highly unlikely you're going to convert someone to you point of view because their beliefs on these issues are so set, and confirmation bias so strong, that you're banging your head against the cognitive bias wall.

How many psychologists does it take to change a light bulb? One, but the lightbulb has got to want to change

That rather old joke explains why change can only occur when a person wants to change. At that point they can abandon confirmation bias and be willing to accept new perceptions. Of course, he or she doesn't abandon confirmation bias, they just use it to justify new perceptions and beliefs.

One of the biggest confirmation bias drivers is romantic "love." Especially in the early stages of a relationship, what in my book *10 Steps to a Great Relationship*, I call the Novel Erotic Attraction (NEA), when we can find nothing wrong with our partners. That is because the feeling is so empowering and wonderful that we don't want to undermine it in any way. Over time, as that high naturally wears off and hopefully transmutes into something more than just a great feeling, the need for everything to be perfect and our feelings not be threatened wanes and we can become more balanced in our view of our partners.

Fear. The avoidance of fear is arguably the most powerful motivator. Research consistently shows there is disproportionate motivation to avoid negative consequences, regardless of how remote they might logically be. **Risk Aversion** is a dominant driver of thinking and as a result, behavior too. The research suggests that this overvaluation in the face of fear is exaggerated by two to three times more than it should be. This level of quantification is made possible using studies where people are given fundamental math problems. For example, people are much more likely to grab the opportunity to not lose $100 than they are to take the opportunity to gain a $100, even though the probabilities are the same.

Environment. The setting in which you perceive an event will influence perception. The same stimulus might be perceived very differently depending on whether you are sitting alone in a church or with a bunch of friends at a party. Have you ever noticed that the culminating and pivotal moments of a movie often occur in a very social setting? **The social environment** is particularly influential; that's why comedy shows have laughter tracks.

There was a famous experiment conducted by psychologist Solomon Asch in the 1950s. If you were a subject in this experiment, you would be asked to decide which of three lines matched a target line. And if you were in the experimental group you would observe several other people making the wrong choice. Would that drive to conformity change your answer? In about a third of cases it did, with subjects choosing the obviously wrong answer simply because they witnessed everyone else doing the same thing. Note, however, that a majority of the subjects were not thus swayed.

Halo Effect. This occurs when we attribute many positive features to someone who has exhibited just one or two of those characteristics. We have a tendency to view anyone we like in an overly positive light, and people we don't in an overly negative light. This is an example of taking minimal knowledge about a thing or person and generalizing it to the whole entity or person. We don't want to turn off the oxytocin, or at least give up the good feelings.

Availability. If we can recall relevant examples to support an idea, we will overvalue those examples. This is where the role of media becomes so important. The media not only chose what stories to cover but *how* to cover them. Moreover, with curation now determining which readers/viewers see what stories, the influence of the media has just gotten even more significant.

The Framing Effect: How a story is framed is critical in how it is perceived. That framing not only is about context but also sensory impressions, too, especially in the media (see Advertising).

Original thought. This is one from my personal experience. My wife and I typically have Sunday brunch at our favorite restaurant. However, on St. Patrick's Day there is a parade, which congregates in the area around the restaurant. On this day I thought it would be a good idea to avoid the restaurant figuring it would be jammed. As luck would have it, we ended up going by it and the place was empty.

"Everyone thinks we're going to be slammed and avoids coming, so we are empty," said the owner.

When we have a thought, it is easy to fall into the trap in thinking that it is an original thought or at least not one shared by many, when often the reality is quite different. A friend of mine used this bias to find a great parking spot in town when he and his son went to see a New England Patriots Superbowl parade. Many people assumed that there would be no parking in the center of town, and parked miles away leaving him free to get a prime parking spot.

I can't claim ownership of the *Original Thought Bias* because although I have not seen it publicized anywhere, it might indeed be and I'm sure many others have had the same idea! This is similar to the *Recency illusion* which is the illusion that comes with believing a phenomenon that one has noticed only recently is itself recent.

Mood.   As we have seen, emotion significantly impacts perception. So, your mood is going to influence perception and thinking in general.

Appeal to Celebrity. Joe Hollywood Star uses this shaving cream so it must be good! Really???

Association with Fame, Power or Greatness
During the 2018 Superbowl, Dodge used a soundtrack of Martin Luther King extolling greatness to sell their trucks! I don't think Martin Luther King had selling trucks in mind when he gave that speech, but the advertiser is trying to associate their product with greatness, ever though the connection is completely spurious. The ad was rightly roundly criticized.

Money.   Just because I spent 1.9 billion dollars researching this book doesn't say anything about the book's value.

Ancient and Long-term practice.   Just because a product or plant has been around and used for centuries doesn't imbue it with some sort of magic. It needs to be based on today's knowledge and science not yesterday's folklore. Sometimes that folklore and knowledge overlap, sometimes they don't.

Appeal to Authority. If someone is a supposed authority on a subject, like a doctor, they must know the truth. While we definitely need to pay attention to someone's qualifications and experience because experts tend to know more than we do, that doesn't mean that experts are always right. First, as far as health and wellness is concerned, a doctor might know a lot about diseases and even treatments, but you are the expert in YOU. And you, and many variables associated with you, are a critical part of effective diagnosis and treatment.

In addition, everyone is biased, especially expert professionals because they were trained in certain models of reality, most of which are approximations, and nearly all of which will change over time.

Need to Conform

The role of other people's opinions can be influential, especially when you work as part of a team with shared missions. Group dynamics can be powerful with a conscious or unconscious need to conform. This can play out in many ways. For example, I have seen it in play of the psychological assessment of people, especially in the legal system.

Let's suppose a health professional has assessed a person and presents evidence that this person is mentally ill in some way. However, there is an objection to the conclusions of the report, so the person is sent for a reassessment. However, the re-assessor is someone who knows the first assessor, works within the same system and moreover, gets their report before conducting their own assessment. Has the re-assessor now been influenced? Of course! In this situation you need a totally independent re-assessor with no access to previous reports to offer an unbiased opinion. Sure, they might be exposed to the same "facts" but not other people's interpretation of them.

You might think that this is a poor example because professionals can and should be independent, regardless of the nature of their relationship with previous assessors. However, mental health assessors are just as subject to cognitive biases as the rest of us.

And now here's a big one...

The *Just World Bias* in which we believe that the world is fair, or should be. While it is a nice dream to imagine a completely fair world, the problem is that what would be fair to one person wouldn't be fair to someone else. Now, this isn't an argument for not trying to rectify obvious unfairness and corruption. However, it is a plea for having realistic views of life.

If you believe that life is, or should be fair, you are going to be mightily disappointed. You are likely to spend much of your life, frustrated and depressed, if not suicidal. You will not learn the effective ways of adapting and being successful. The strength and power of each of us is that we can, if we choose, find growth, meaning and purpose by rising to the challenges we face in an unfair world. The secret isn't complaining about unfairness, it is creatively and successfully adapting to it.

Here are some other common biases.

Bias blind spot. This is an important one. It refers to the tendency to see oneself as less biased than others, or to identify more cognitive biases in other people.

Courtesy bias. The tendency to give a politically correct opinion rather than your true opinion, to avoid offending anyone.

Declinism. The predisposition to view the past more favorably and the future negatively. This certainly can be a factor as we age despite the fact that many people think of their later years as fulfilling.

Default effect. The tendency to favor the default, more conservative choice.

DeWaal Effect: The tendency to overvalue human capacities and undervalue animal ones.

Dunning–Kruger effect. The tendency for the unskilled to overestimate their ability and for experts to underestimate theirs.

Exaggerated expectation. The tendency to expect overly extreme outcomes.

Focusing effect. Exaggerating the importance of one aspect of an event.

Framing effect. Being influenced by how information is presented. Recall the memory studies mentioned earlier that showed how events were described significantly influenced perception. This is definitely a key to "fake news".

Gambler's fallacy. This is the notion that future probabilities are altered by past events, when logically there is no influence because the events are independent. For example, if you toss a coin ten times and it lands on heads each time, the assumption that the odds of it being tails on the eleventh toss are now significantly enhanced is a fallacy. Any time a coin is tossed the odds are 50:50.

Groupthink. This occurs when the desire for group cohesion leads to poor decision-making. By minimizing intra-group conflict, members may not fully explore all alternatives.

Hindsight bias. This is the tendency to look back at past events and see them as predictable at the time they occurred. Have you ever said to yourself, "I knew it all along"?

Hostile attribution bias. This is the tendency to interpret other people as having hostile intent, in spite of very little or any evidence to support the notion.

Hot-hand fallacy. This is the belief that when a person is on a "hot streak" that it will continue. For example, a basketball player with a career shooting average of 40%, hits ten shots in a row and the team then try to get him the ball for every shot.

Hyperbolic discounting. This is the tendency for people to prefer immediate payoffs relative to later payoffs.

Illusion of control. This is the overestimation of one's influence over external events.

Illusion of validity. This is the tendency to believe that our judgments are accurate, despite inconsistent or unavailable information.

Illusory correlation. Inaccurately seeing a relationship between two unrelated variables or events. This is critical aspect of pseudoscience.

Illusory truth effect. Believing that a statement is true when it is easier to understand, or if it has been stated many times, independent of its validity.

Interoceptive bias. The tendency to interpret sensory information as evidence of external or internal reality. See the falling in love examples mentioned earlier. This is a core concept in Offendology.

The Sunk Cost Fallacy. When we justify putting more money (or any resources) into a project based on what has already been spent rather that a rational analysis of the probability of success.

Negativity bias. We have a tendency to more clearly recall negative memories than positive ones.

Neglect of probability. Disregarding probability when making a decision that is complicated.

Normalcy bias. The refusal to accurately consider planning for, or reacting to, a seriously negative event that has never happened before. (see Brexit, Climate Change).

Optimism bias. The tendency to overestimate pleasing outcomes.

Pessimism bias. The tendency to overestimate negative outcomes.

Planning fallacy. The tendency to underestimate the time it takes to complete a task.

Post-purchase rationalization. Persuading oneself that a purchase was good value.

Present bias. The tendency to favor current rather than future payoffs

Pro-innovation bias. An unverified optimism about an invention or innovation's value simply because it is new, while failing to recognize its limitations and weaknesses.

Projection bias. The tendency to assume our future selves will share our current preferences, thoughts and values.

Reactance. Doing the opposite of what someone asks you to do on the rationalization that you don't want to be seen as having your freedom of choice constrained. (See Regression in the defense mechanisms).

Reactive devaluation. Discrediting proposals simply because you think they were devised by an adversary.

Recency illusion. The tendency to think that just because *you* have noticed something for the first time, it must be a recent development.

Regressive bias. The exaggeration of high values and probabilities, and the minimizing of low values and probabilities.

Restraint bias.   Overestimating your ability to resist temptation.

Social desirability bias.   The tendency to over-report your socially desirable characteristics and under-report undesirable ones.

And finally, perhaps one of the more important ones…

Naïve realism.   The belief that we see reality as it really is. We are objective and the facts are obvious and those that disagree are obviously uninformed, lazy, irrational and certainly biased.

"Real Knowledge is to know the extent of one's ignorance." – Confucius

Questions
1. Are you aware of when a cognitive bias is in play?
2. Do you recognize your own cognitive bias?
3. Are you prone to use one bias more than others?
4. Are you prone to be influenced by one bias more than another?

Chapter Twelve

Bias and Spirituality

No wonder God was so annoyed with Adam and Eve from eating of the Tree of Knowledge. He knew that Man now didn't have the cognitive apparatus to understand knowledge and would, therefore, use a small amount of knowledge to fuel story-telling and assumption-laden narratives. And to make matters worse, Man would think he understood, when in fact he only got a very small part of the picture.

This was evident as soon as God asked Adam why he had eaten from the Tree of Knowledge when he had been forbidden to do so.

"Eve, made me do it," said Adam. Well, duh, God saw what happened. He knew who encouraged whom. Moreover, not only did Adam say that Eve made me do it he told God, that "the woman you made" made me do it. See, it was God's fault! And then Eve said that it was the serpent that God made that made her do it so, again, it was God's fault.

And thus it started. Entire eons would pass during which humans avoided the question by giving an irrelevant answer: they perfected the art of deflection. Adam hadn't answered the question, a perfect demonstration of an emotional, narrative-driven response rather than rational explanation. And, to cap it off, he projected his guilt back on God

Reflection not deflection or projection!

If Adam had reflected rather than deflected, he would have been able to give a better answer, which goes something like this: "I am sorry, God. I am a disobedient servant who couldn't exercise control over the one thing you asked me not to do. " If he had been that authentic, Adam might have been able to add something like,

"If there's still time, Lord, perhaps could you tweak my frontal lobes so I can do better next time?"

Speaking of God, it is apparent from what you have read so far, that thinking isn't just about algebraic equations or esoteric formulae. Your thinking is a reflection of, and significantly influenced by, your soul. It's about your moral values, about who you are as a person. That's why the mature, adaptive defense mechanisms are rooted in moral and beneficent values. So, spirituality in all its forms is not just about   respecting others and yourself, it is the basis of your emotional management and thus your thinking. As I wrote in *Power Talk...*

Spirituality is the opposite of narcissism

It's useful to consider the seven deadly sins and their opposite graces.

Lust	Chastity
Gluttony	Temperance
Greed	Charity
Sloth	Diligence
Wrath	Patience
Envy	Gratitude
Pride	Humility

If you live mainly in the left-hand column, you will misguided, biased and mostly irrational.

You will put others down to build yourself up.

You will live in a frenzy of emotion, mostly anger, hate, frustration and depression.

Your thought process will be egocentric.

You will be constantly seeking excuses and finding them in other people.

You will feel a victim but the louder you shout and complain, the less you are likely to get the love you are craving.

Codes of ethics and behavior driven by authentic spiritual principles don't brainwash people. On the contrary, they allow people who practice the principles appropriately, to be open-minded and to think with clarity and without as much bias. It is why all the sages and wise people in history were, first and foremost, spiritual beings.

We have seen that one of the problems with thinking is that we have a tough time with relativity. In addition, we can't possibly remember all the relevant experiences that we have had. Oh, and that the experiences that do influence us might be unconscious, leading to emotions that we don't really understand or know how to attribute or scale. Oh, and we can't possibly know all the variables -- even the ones we can think about. Oh, and we can't possibly know all the variables that we haven't even thought about. As we go higher up the scale of consciousness and enlightenment, the more these limitations are presumed to fade away. Then we get to a higher power, who is one hell of a multi-tasker because He or She knows everything all at the same time!

That is the appeal of a higher power. We recognize the limitations of the human mind and can see the possibilities at the far side of the knowledge continuum; a force that can be all-knowing.

Now, there are undoubtedly many people who would argue that a belief in a God is simply a bias aimed at making us more comfortable with uncertainty, an attempt to find control and meaning in an increasingly unpredictable world.

That's not an unreasonable proposition. One interesting aspect of this phenomenon is that, at least currently, we can't find a way to objectively prove the presence of this higher power, although that would be disputed by some, who might, for example, point to the seeming miracle of nature. For now, though, it has to remain a belief.

Now, there might be several reasons for being an atheist, and lack of 'evidence' of a God may be one of them. However, as they say in science, *the absence of evidence does not mean evidence of absence.* It just means we don't "know".

Personally, I believe in a higher power for several reasons.

10 Reasons to Believe in a Higher Power

1. It's a reminder that we're not as awesome as we like to think
2. It helps get us out of our own individual egos and recognize that we part of a much greater system of nature
3. It helps focus us on cooperation and interdependence, which I believe are necessary for humanity and the species in general
4. By reminding us of our weaknesses, it helps us focus on self-improvement
5. It provides a moral compass. Numerous business and success gurus stress the importance of keeping our goals in front of us and focusing on them every day. Where else do you get that moral guidance? Not in the culture, for sure.
6. It's a reminder that we can't predict the future, and that almost anything is possible. It can give hope.
7. It keeps us vigilant about materialism – both forms. Here I'm referring to two forms of materialism. There's economic materialism, and then there's the philosophical materialism and the determinism that derives from it that I have mentioned elsewhere in this book. We shouldn't put

possessions before virtue nor have a philosophical addiction to the material world.

8. It encourages emotional control; "the meek shall inherit the earth".
9. It encourages refraining from judgment
10. It guards against hypocrisy; "forgive us our trespasses as we forgive those who trespass against us…"

Of course, you can embrace all these points without necessarily believing in a higher power, but to me that would seem a lot harder to do without a supreme being, but it definitely is a very viable position. However, if you don't believe in a higher power, where do you get your moral and spiritual teaching? You might be fortunate enough to live in an amazingly spiritual and moral family and a microculture that supports and teaches the important foundations, but what if you are not, or worse still live in a microculture that teaches the complete opposite, like narcissism?

The issue here is not a label. My respect for someone is based on who they are as a person, not which church they do or don't go to. Somebody who doesn't subscribe to a particular church might in fact be living life in accordance with the principles espoused by Jesus. I try not to stereotype and engage in binary thinking

Iceberg Thinking Revisited
Emotions drive thinking and exaggerate. The first thing that comes into your mind is almost certainly going to be an overstatement, exaggeration and not representative of a complex reality. It's a knee jerk response. The question is whether you then bother with the laborious process of trying to dig deeper to unravel the complexity or take the easy way out and just buy into your first impression. It is like seeing just the tip of the iceberg and ignoring what might be below the surface. And it's what's below the surface that will get you.

Of course, there are gradations of this process. For example, that first impression is likely to "anchor" your thought process, and influence your exploration of it, even if you don't accept it outright. The reality is that if you can manipulate a perception or facts to conform to an emotionally consistent and satisfactory narrative, you'll probably stop there. In fact, your analytic process will likely be geared to being able to rationalize your perceptions and create the narrative that you want as quickly as possible.

The higher power hopefully helps you escape from this narcissistic process and provide you with a perspective that makes you open to different narratives that may be emotionally uncomfortable and even inconsistent with your beliefs. That is one definition of enlightenment and enhanced consciousness -- a willingness to step outside the comfort of your own narratives and be open to reshaping them. This willingness to change narratives, ideas and beliefs seems in serious decline. I believe it is one of the frustrations that people have with politicians, who seemed to be committed to ideology and party "machinery" rather than a rational assessment of complex situations. Of course, most people can't escape their own narratives either.

Most spiritual teachings center around the process of being able to step outside the confines of narcissistic narratives and be willing to entertain other perspectives and experiences, though not necessarily to endorse or agree with them. In the broadest sense this requires love, compassion and the suspension of kneejerk thinking, which is why these characteristics are at the heart of spiritual growth.

Your Lower Power

As we go up the scale of enlightenment and consciousness and escape the biases of the binary brain, reason and prediction become much more accurate. Conversely, as we go down the scale of consciousness and enlightenment the problems of rationalization and rationality get a whole lot worse. And unfortunately, the

Lower Power is very popular and influential -- indeed, powerful. The Lower Power consists of emotions like rage, anger, frustration, stress, that can all easily over-ride rationality and any attempt to really understand complexity but rather 'shape the narrative.'

For a very long time indeed, humans have known that to influence and persuade others to do things, like buy their products or go to war, you need to appeal to inherent cognitive biases. Any self-respecting communication expert will tell you that if you generate the right emotion -- be that fear or joy -- you can pass off anything as rational. Emotion not reason is the key to a winning message. What that means in an increasingly marketing society that...

The prime form of communication is emotional manipulation not reason.

And because marketing is the biggest form of communication, we are surrounded and seduced by the model that eventually has us believing that narrative and emotional persuasion are the same as, or even more important than, rational argument. Few people are interested in facts or data, unless, of course, they are emotionally consistent with their beliefs and goals. Moreover, marketing is designed to cater to the needs of an individual, elevating the importance of the individual to himself and in the overall context of the culture.

Advertising is legalized lying -- H.G. Wells

Advertising can be very subversive. Consider the typical pharmaceutical ad. While describing the drug's benefits, you see images of smiling people and hear soft music, both of which elicit positive, calm feelings. Then, per regulatory compliance, a list of the drug's side-effects is mentioned. However, while this list of negative effects is being described, often at high speed, the same pleasing images and soft music continue to embrace our senses, significantly influencing the perception and cognitive analysis of the side-effects. Surely this is wrong?

When being told of the side-effects shouldn't we see images of people experiencing those exact side-effects rather than soothing images that blunt the perception and comprehension of those symptoms? Shouldn't we see people throwing up, if nausea is a side-effect? Shouldn't we hear the loud wailing of ambulance sirens rushing to someone we have just seen collapse with a heart attack, if that is a potential side-effect? Shouldn't we see someone being buried if death is a potential side-effect? Shouldn't we see people still taking the same pills ten years later because withdrawing from them is so difficult? If the goal was a balanced, rational view of the medication's possibilities, that's exactly what we should see but this is an advertisement designed to sell you a product and make it seem as beneficial as possible.

Seen that way, advertising can be seen to be very subversive. Perhaps as you think about this you might find yourself getting angry at the sheer manipulation. However, don't most of us communicate like that -- emphasizing what we want and minimizing what we don't? And because of anchoring and other biases, it is easy to accept this type of communication. And in defense of pharmaceutical ads, if the side effects are way, way less common than the main effects, perhaps they shouldn't be given the same prominence? It's that problem of scaling again.

However, at a time when the role of lifestyle behaviors like eating are shown to be major influences on health one has to question the role of marketing that encourages ill health and disease. For example, the estimated direct and indirect costs of diabetes in the USA in 2012 was estimated at $245 billion.
https://www.cdc.gov/diabetes/data/statistics-report/deaths-cost.html

Sodas and sugary drinks are just one gateway to excessive sugar consumption and diabetes. In 2017 Coca-Cola spent an estimated $900 million in US advertising.

https://www.statista.com/statistics/286526/coca-cola-advertising-spending-worldwide/

In the same year Pepsi spent $170 million in advertising just the Pepsi brand.

https://www.statista.com/statistics/286547/pepsico-advertising-spending-worldwide/

Of course, not everyone who drinks soda is going to get diabetes and not everyone who has diabetes drank soda. However, it is a contributor to a major and expensive health problem.

Bias and Technology
I have the privilege of working with Grant Renier at Intuality (www.intuialityAI.com). Grant and his colleagues have devised predictive technology not solely based on logic but the way the biased brain really thinks, allowing it to more accurately predict anything from financial markets to sports, from consumer choices to health behavior. The analytics take into account twelve key biases. Intuality has the capability of looking at data sets that go back several years with and without individual cognitive biases built into the predictive technology. The preliminary research suggests that over that time, cognitive bias is associated with greater predictive accuracy suggesting that over the last quarter of a century we may have become more "fast and frugal" and less attentive to more complex rational analysis. This would hardly be surprising given the amount of information that people now process daily and the time available for serious logical thinking.

So, for a variety of reasons, which include technology, activism, political correctness and educational practice, the ability to see the limitations of the binary brain and cognitive bias might be getting worse. In the era of the selfie, objectivity is getting a downgrade.

Homo Sapiens
I can hear you now.

"Howard, you are being way too harsh on the human race. It has produced amazing technological understanding and advance."

You are guilty of an *over-inclusion bias* here. The fact is that I would have been no more likely than my dog to have discovered electricity, the telephone, the internet, relativity and all the other technological and scientific advances that Man gets credit for -- and, no offense, but I suspect you wouldn't have, either. 99.999 (I could go on here but you get the point) per cent of humans don't advance the human race in terms of knowledge or technology -- a few really smart people do.

Some of those really smart, game-changing people (e.g. Einstein) had brains that were different from the norm. However, it is unclear whether Einstein started off with a different brain, or it became shaped that way because of his thought process. As we'll see later, the brain is very plastic and not only eminently capable of this type of change, but adaptation is its hallmark. However, for me or any other ordinary mortal to group myself with Einstein, or Tesla, or Edison, is highly questionable. All of us are just plain lucky that we are on the same team as Einstein, Tesla or Edison. However, this raises a critical point about humans.

It is possible to become more like those technological wizards and advance the human race when we are able to master our Lower Power and advance on the consciousness scale. When that happens…

We can all make life better for everyone not just ourselves

The fact is homo needs to get more sapiens.

God's End-of Semester Report Card.
It's important to know that His school is based on the following verse:

Corinthians 1: 13:13
Three things will last forever -- faith, hope and love -- and the greatest of these is love. (Note that rationality and rationalizations don't make the top three)

Semester ending 6/12/2019
Dogs: A+   Always humble, know their limitations and epitomize love. Well done!

Dolphins: A   Empathic, smart and loving. Excellent semester!

Humans: D+   Arrogant bullies who think they know everything when in fact they know very little. Need significant improvement. I feel another flood coming on.

Questions
1. When you are discussing an issue do you resort to bias to justify your behavior?
2. How would you confront someone using bias as justification for their actions?
3. Are you aware of what stage of cognitive development you're operating on?

Chapter Thirteen

Intuition

Now the astute reader might at this point be saying something to the effect: "I agree that thinking is flawed and that's why I often go with my gut when I make decisions." But what is intuition and where does it fit into the process of thinking and decision-making?

Intuition is a feeling. You might get a "feeling" that something isn't right, or on the contrary, that a situation is absolutely wonderful. But what is this feeling and how do you evaluate it?

Many years ago, while I was in clinical practice, I had a client with a severe dissociative disorder or what used to be called Multiple Personality Disorder. She had an incredibly traumatic upbringing with severe abuse by both parents. What I learned while working with her is that each of her many alter egos were tied to one, or one class, of traumatic events. Each alter ego held the memory of that class of trauma, and this was not "shared" in consciousness because it was simply too overwhelming. As a result, there was a hierarchy of alter egos, organized around specific traumas and degrees of emotional severity: from shame to total terror.

At various times, different alter egos would appear with their specific physical, emotional and behavioral symptoms. For example, the client came to me one day complaining of a terrible migraine that she simply couldn't get rid of, even with the strongest medication. I knew from her history which alter ego that was, and using hypnotic techniques was able to push that particular alter ego out of consciousness. When the client came back to reality about fifteen minutes later, she looked stunned and delighted.

"My migraine has gone!" she exclaimed.

Each alter ego was associated with a specific class of traumas and had developed   physical, emotional and behavioral characteristics specific to her experiences and memories.

Now, in some ways, this dissociation was an incredibly adaptive survival mechanism, preventing the client from being persecuted by constant thoughts and feelings of horror, shame, guilt and deadly threats.

The secret to effective treatment was to uncover these buried and hidden experiences and memories and bring them to consciousness where they could be addressed and defused. Once into consciousness, there was no longer need for them to be hidden and kept separate and so these alter egos disappeared. The key was to unpeel the traumatic onion, pulling back the layers and layers of trauma and dissociated defenses.

When uncovering a new alter ego and the trauma therein, the client at first might consciously feel nothing when talking about them. Eventually though, more and more emotion would return, defining itself more fully. At first, there might be nothing, then a sense of unease and then full-blown emotion as the alter ego and the trauma underpinning it emerged from the fog of repression.

Research also showed me that there is a neurological basis for the emergence of "unemotional" recall of terrifying experiences. The brain recruits the different parts of the memory and puts them together as a whole. But those different parts, like the emotion associated with the experience, are housed in the brain independently. Thus, a memory could be partially recalled without the emotional component, at least at first. Or one could feel the emotion but not have an understanding of where it came from or what it was about.

It took us twelve years to effectively unpeel the whole onion. As I learned about this condition over the years, I realized that Multiple

Personality Disorder was a confusing term. What I saw was a *fragmented* personality, not multiple ones. I saw someone who was fragmented because of multiple traumas.

Now, we all have memories and experiences locked away in our unconscious. Because there's no trauma attached to them, they are not forbidden to emerge, but they are not accessed for one reason or another. This is the 'fringe of consciousness' and it runs deeper than the fringe. And as with my client described above, you might have a feeling but have no idea where it is coming from.

For example, one of my client's traumas was associated with a certain type of flower. Prior to therapy, without knowledge of this association, she would always feel strangely fearful when she saw these flowers but was not aware enough at that point of their significance -- their connection to a traumatic event. She would say she had a vibe about them, or even the place where they were, and simply avoided them. Call it intuition if you want. It was the feeling of dread without any known reason why she should feel that dread.

Now various things can arouse these hidden feelings and memories. Any sense impression can elicit discomfort or delight depending on its unconscious associations. However, *without knowing those associations, there's no way of working out whether the feelings are based in reality and should be taken as real warning signs, or are merely spurious associations.*

For example, you go for a job interview and the woman who interviews you makes you feel uncomfortable. Rationally, you can find no reason for your discomfort, it's just there. What does it mean?

Well, it could mean almost anything, and your discomfort could be based on all sorts of cues. For example, unconsciously her eyes are reminding you of a schoolmate who badly betrayed you. Hmm, that does not sound like a good reason to mistrust her and potentially turn down a good job offer. Yet, you walk away feeling that something is not quite right.

Maybe your unease with her was a projection of your own discomfort and nothing to do with the interviewer?

Or alternatively, she touched her nose a lot while talking. You don't know this, but that actually is a sign of lying and you might be simply deducing that from interactions with other people who you couldn't trust. Or she might just have an itchy nose. Who knows?

My point is that these shapeless feelings, which most people describe as intuition, can be legitimate reasons to drive thinking and behavior, or they can be the result of spurious and meaningless associations with other experiences. These feelings will certainly drive the narrative, but the question is whether that narrative is legitimate or not.

Interestingly, there is a very strong connection between the gut and the brain, and it's called the enteric nervous system. It is so powerful that the gut is often called the "second brain." Indeed, the gut has as many as 30 neurotransmitters that are found in the brain. Not only are the ingredients needed for making some of the key neurotransmitters found in the gut, some are more prevalent in the gut than in the brain. For example, 90% of serotonin (the transmitter that has been targeted in the medication treatment of depression) and 50% of the dopamine is there, too. Dopamine is a major neurotransmitter involved in motivation, rewards and pleasure.

The enteric nervous system can operate independently of the autonomic nervous system, but they also work in harmony. And there's something else that might be critical to health and certainly part of the mind-body connection.

The gut has millions of various microbes and bacteria that contribute to health, wellbeing and also illness. The gut environment is controlled by the enteric nervous system, which therefore plays a large role in determining which bacteria and microbes thrive and survive and which die. And that will determine our health and wellbeing.

Thus, there's an established mechanism by which our gut can influence our feelings, and thus our thoughts. It's no surprise then, that we take notice of our gut reactions. However, we still need to try to understand the basis of those reactions so we can evaluate them and determine whether they are genuine markers of something important that we are not yet conscious of or are, alternatively, unconscious spurious associations with past experiences which have little significance on their own.

Questions
1. Do you regularly go with your gut reactions?
2. Can you recall a time when you did and were subsequently proven right?
3. Can you recall a time when you didn't and were subsequently proven right?

Chapter Fourteen

Cognitive Bias and Fake News in Daily Life

As the concept of cognitive bias and the ways we really think become better known, more work is done in different areas of society applying these concepts. One of the best applications of bias can be found in Adam Benforado's excellent book *Unfair: the New Science of Criminal Injustice.* In it, Benforado looks at how bias affects the legal process, often using real life case examples.

There are some examples, which are frightful and an affront to anyone who thinks that the legal system must be fair. For example, there's the practice of offering a potential defendant a much shorter sentence for a crime that he didn't commit, just to get a conviction. For example, a poor immigrant who was near the crime scene is told that if he goes to trial the jury will probably be against him from the beginning and he could be looking at forty years inside. Just admit the crime and take the three years imprisonment. Probably be out in two. What would you do?

Or what about the practice of not pursuing legal action against the very rich because they have the resources to drain the prosecutor's office time, energy and money by prolonging the process until they force the prosecutor to give up.

Judges are also subject to biases: they are only human. There's the evidence that judges sentencing got harsher the more tired and hungry they became. These factors are much more likely to effect decision-making that occurs over a short term than long term decision-making where, presumably, the influence of such variables as fatigue, mood and hunger will be less likely to have an effect. That's one reason why it is always good to wait a day or so to review critical decisions. You might see them differently on a full stomach, or after a great night's sleep.

But beyond the examples of how the system works, there is the whole issue of cognitive bias. Jurors will have their perceptions and thus their conclusions influenced by a variety of cues, which can be overrated. For example, unattractive people tend to get longer sentences than attractive ones. The literature on beauty is fairly clear that, in general, attractive people are assumed to have more positive attributes than unattractive people.

The way a defendant or witness sits, the clothes they wear, their body language, all convey certain things which may not reflect reality. For example, a confident witness will probably be seen as more honest than a bumbling one. Information gained from actually seeing the person will influence the jury and this can create the wrong impression about a witness.

Benforado suggests that based on his experience and research, it would be better if jurors did not see defendants and witnesses at all, to prevent them from being overly influenced by these biasing factors. His suggestion is that jurors just see written testimony to prevent them from being overly biased by the usual judgmental factors that come into play when you actually see someone.

Then there is the whole problem of witnesses accepting a deal to escape punishment by telling their side of the story that will convict others. How reliable is that testimony? If someone has a compelling reason to create a narrative, that benefit will surely influence how the story is told and how it is presented. One could certainly imagine a witness convincing himself or herself of events when it is advantageous to do so, let alone outright lying to get themselves out of a jam (or make money). Some of these people would actually come to believe a story that they concocted.

During the time of writing this, the Brett Kavanaugh confirmation hearings were in progress and Prof Christy Ford has made accusations about Kavanaugh's behavior. Of course, people have made up their own mind about "who is telling the truth" based on their own narratives and personal beliefs.

First, I couldn't begin to make a judgment because I do not have all the relevant information, and even if I did, I would have doubt about the reliability of that information, not because of either of the two people involved but because of the processes of memory and perception mentioned in this book. The fact is that in a case like this, neither of them can objectively know "what really happened" because time, circumstances and the other variables mentioned in this book come into play. Of course, there may be blatant false statements that can be disproved, but in many such cases, we have unreliable memory of a biased perception, possibly on both sides.

For example, let's suppose a young couple are making out. There's a consensus to take it further into intercourse. They start into the first stage. The girl suddenly gets agitated. She's not sure why, but she begins to feel uncomfortable. She tries to work out what she is feeling. Eventually, the guy sees his lover is uncomfortable and stops and asks what's wrong. She's not sure but she believes she is having memories of being abused. The guy comforts her as she starts to cry. Then she suddenly gets up and goes into the shower.

How will each of these people recall this event in the future? As we have seen, the memory is not a video recorder. It can change. Future events, context and a host of other variables will determine how each will recall this. It's not anyone's fault, it's the nature of how the mind works. We just need to recognize the limitations.

Outside the issues of plaintiffs and defendants, there are the attorneys themselves. The way they dress, talk and generally conduct themselves convey attributes that may or may not be appropriately valued. As a writer, I have seen advertisements for freelancer writers to write books about how to be effective as an attorney. One group of actors clearly makes a good living out of coaching attorneys in how to conduct themselves more effectively: from how they dressed to how they approached the jury, from the words they used to how they examined witnesses. Of course, we would hope that the legal system wasn't so open to bias, but based on Benforado's work, one can see that is a misguided hope. And of course, it's a legal system not a justice system. In other words, it is based on interpretation of the laws, not morality. One hopes that there's some correspondence between the laws and morality, but again, there are limitations on how well words can define all the possible perceptions of a behavior.

Mental health assessments in particular are vulnerable to cognitive bias. I am familiar with one case where a father was trying to retain rights to the visitation of his pre-teen daughter. Unfortunately, he was not a good communicator and had some question marks on his record but his heart was definitely in the right place and he loved his daughter; the amount of time and money he invested in trying to keep his visitation rights was a testimony to that commitment to his daughter. However, the murky issues around him, conspired to make those assessing him see him as a threat to his daughter. They dragged out all sorts of conspiratorial ideas to make the guy look very shady. And, of course, they favored the mother, despite the fact she had a very high lie score on the MMPI, (which meant that everything she said should be viewed with extreme caution), hit her child and was clearly an unreliable witness prone to total exaggeration.

The family court in particular is prone to the vagaries of cognitive bias. When it gets to that stage of the legal process, emotions are running high on both sides, influencing the narratives, as well as memories and perceptions. And the fact is that some people are very convincing in their stories.

Medical Bias

As in the legal system, bias pops up all over the place in the medical system, too. As we have seen, science can only give us the best estimates at the current time, in full expectation that these will be influenced by later research and might some day even be discredited completely. However, medical research and its implications are often seen as definitive facts rather than current probabilities. So, we might view a condition as fatal when, in fact, 15% of people don't actually die from the disease.

There are many examples of people making extraordinary recoveries from supposedly fatal conditions. The book that I co-wrote with Barbara Morello O'Donnell, *In God's Waiting Room* tells of Barb's miraculous healing after a series of spiritual experiences. We need to be careful about how we convey so-called "terminal" illnesses. The more detail that we can give about the known probabilities of a particular condition, the better. If 15% of people actually survive the condition, we can offer that as a beacon of hope as well as understanding what factors might be associated with recovery.

This becomes more problematic when the diagnosis for a medical condition is based on where someone is on a continuum.

Let's take obstructive sleep apnea (OSA), which is characterized by an obstruction to airflow, leading to episodes of waking and sleep disruption.

Michael Semelka, Jonathan Wilson and Ryan Floyd describe the diagnostic process...

"Sleep studies performed in a sleep laboratory or in the home can quantify the apnea-hypopnea index, which is required to diagnose OSA. Apnea is a complete obstruction of airflow, and hypopnea is a partial obstruction of airflow; both must last a minimum of 10 seconds. Hypopneas are measured by oxygen desaturation of 3% or more or arousal from sleep. The apnea-hypopnea index is calculated by adding all apneas and hypopneas and then dividing by total sleep time. An apnea-hypopnea index of 15 or more events per hour, or five or more events per hour in the presence of symptoms or cardiovascular comorbidities, is diagnostic for OSA."

So, what if your apnea/hypopnea index is 10 not 15, or you have only 3 events per hour in the presence of other symptoms? Does that mean you don't have OSA? I certainly can imagine someone falling outside of the official diagnostic code numbers, being told that they have the problem, need to get help, need to get a C-PAP machine and so on. Is that good medical practice or creating an unnecessary dependency?

I used to co-host a radio show called Master Your Life, with Canadian health and wellness coach, Leaha Mattinson.

Leaha is a testament to an adaptive approach to a medical issue. Diagnosed as gene-positive for the genetic Huntington's Disease, Leaha said, "This is not for me." She wasn't ignoring the diagnosis, far from it. What she was avoiding were the biases and assumptions implicit in the diagnosis, specifically that she would inevitably develop symptoms in the next few years.

Leaha learned all she could about the disease and then set about adapting the healthiest behaviors possible. She is still symptom-free, very vital and never gets sick.

Beyond these examples, there is something more biased and damaging with the medical system, especially in the US.

The system is focused on illness and symptom relief rather than prevention and wellness. This creates the biased notion that illness is something that happens to us, rather than a function of our choices and lifestyles that we can actually control. This is a huge disconnect as the research quite consistently tells us that illness and even diseases such as Alzheimer's are a function of lifestyle behaviors. Dean and Ayesha Sherzai's *The Alzheimer's Solution* states that 90% of AD could be significantly delayed if not avoided altogether by the adoption of healthy lifestyles.

Given the model outlined in this book about how we think, how can we view, for example, the prescription of anti-depressant medications?

Let's take someone who is depressed. They have little energy. Thoughts are mostly lacking any drive or positive elements. They see the world as a dark place.

In the model described in this book, that person's perceptions are driven by past experiences as well as context and culture. In the case of someone who has had a difficult past, or who has learned to interpret events negatively, or both, the perception will drive both a dark narrative and the physiology of hopelessness and these two will reinforce each other in an almost unbreakable bond.

If the person is prescribed an anti-depressant, it might modulate the physical response. They might have a little more energy. However, will that be enough to change the narrative? Could it be that the person still has a depressed narrative and outlook but a moderated emotional response to it? In that case medication has attenuated the physiological response but hasn't changed the narrative, especially if the person reasonably attributes the less negative emotional response to an external factor -- the meds. Has anything changed or we do simply have a reduction in the negative emotion and not the negative mindset?

Now, it could also be, that the attenuation of the emotional response, in the right context, e.g. therapy, support, etc., allows the person to rearrange their narratives and become more "positive." However, one concern in this scenario is that the person will feel the need to be on medication indefinitely for fear that in a unmedicated state their negative physiological response will return, igniting more negative narratives.

What other medical conditions and treatments are based on part truths or no truth at all? Type II diabetes can be reversed and certainly slowed by significant changes to diet. Would more people take this course of action if there were no medications available to treat the diabetes symptoms?

When you see illness as something that is external that happens to you, you will turn to treatments that will fix or manage the problem, like drugs, rather than adopt healthier lifestyle behaviors. It's not that those are mutually exclusive alternatives, of course, but why wait until you're sick to do something about your unhealthy behavior? Moreover, there is a tendency to think that a medication has fixed the problem whereas it has, in most cases, mitigated the symptoms.

However, perhaps the biggest bias that influences health is temporal discounting. We are very poor at projecting into the future and as a result can easily blow off other people's concerns about our future health. We eat the junk food now because it is more pleasing and because of our disconnect with the future impact of it. We need to find ways to help people overcome temporal discounting, which would make preventive medicine way more powerful. There is more about this in the How Not To Think workbook.

Organizations and Leadership
In any organization, there will be various agendas that may or may not be related to the mission statement. Regardless of the intent of the agenda, it is likely to bias perception and thinking. This person thinks that strategy A is best for the company, whereas this person thinks that it is strategy B, and yet another executive thinks it is strategy C. What is needed is creative thinking about each

strategy, which involves not seeing them in a binary way as mutually exclusive alternatives. This would involve recognizing and limiting various biases such as *groupthink*, the *normalcy bias*, the *distinction bias*, the *courtesy effect*, and many, many more!

More recently, corporations have encouraged creative, out of the box, thinking because they see its importance and value. The days when the prevailing philosophy was that there is only one way of doing things has begun to subside and organizations are realizing the massive, irreplaceable value of creativity and non-binary thinking (see the dangers of the **Normalcy bias**). As the world has moved away from convention and towards innovation, the necessity of creating a co-operative, interdependent and problem-solving mindset has become clear. The responsibility for this falls on leadership to recognize the importance of this culture at every level of the organization.

Often the term "emotional intelligence" is touted as a key leadership behavior. This recognizes the importance of the leader's recognition that emotions, both her own and that of her organizational members, need to be effectively managed to prevent the outbreak of false narratives and discontent. But another part of emotional control, as we have seen, is that such control typically allows for more creativity and non-binary thinking.

Organizational rigidity often comes in the form of bureaucracy. In order to standardize a procedure or a practice, bureaucrats have to turn to determinism and binary thinking to create the rules.

Bureaucracy
In order to provide a standardized framework for people to operate under, it is necessary in many walks of life to create the rules. As we have seen, life is complex. The same behaviors can be seen quite differently depending on context. A guy exceeding the speed limit trying to get his sick baby to the hospital is considered as guilty as someone fleeing the scene of a crime. Many times

bureaucracy is therefore, a testimony to the *human weakness of being unable to accurately define context*. That's why bureaucracy often seems so absurd and unfair; it tries to categorize behaviors in different contexts as the same behavior. Bureaucratic behavior is indeed a great testimony to the critical importance of context in understanding the *meaning of the behavior* rather than just considering the behavior.

Cognitive bias impacts every aspect of life, because it is how humans think.

Education
In conventional education, logic and rationality were taught in subjects such as math and science where logical systems need to be understood. However, while STEM subjects do teach logic and rationality, it is not clear how these can generalize to thinking in general and it is not only the way to teach people how to reason.

We need different ways of teaching about thinking, and thinking about teaching.

This is not about understanding algebra or complex equations. It is about understanding the simplistic way in which we think and being aware that emotion, the environment and other factors significantly influence our thought process, perceptions and judgments. Don't you think that a course in how the human mind really works and how to manage your thinking would be valuable?

How about a course in logic using real world examples, rather than esoteric symbolic mathematical equations? For example, an exercise in compounding would look like this.

Students are given one token each day and told that the amount they are given will double every day. The tokens, are exchangeable for different "prizes." One group of students, group A, are on the token program for a week (5 school days), another for two weeks

(10 school days). At the end of the first week, group A are allowed to trade in their tokens. Wow, they have 31 tokens! The other group have to wait until the end of the second week to trade in their tokens. They have 1023!!!

Understanding numbers is important in intelligently considering many problems. For example, a comprehension of numbers is needed for an understanding of an economy. Many people have grand plans for one pet peeve or another but give absolutely zero attention to the costs of such plans.

A piece by Adrienne Bernhard in July 2018 addressed this problem.
http://www.bbc.com/capital/story/20180706-why-it-matters-if-we-become-innumerate

"People who are innumerate cannot calculate the value of a 25% off sale or split the bar tab with friends. They are unable to compare two retirement plans or choose between two mortgages or even two differently sized cans of soda. They may confuse large or small orders of magnitude, fixate on certain risks, mistake correlation for causality or see meaningless patterns in random events. Innumeracy may even affect how you vote."

"And the problem seems to be getting worse. Roughly four in every five adults in the UK struggle with mathematical literacy. The mean numeracy proficiency scores of 16-65 year-olds in the US is significantly below average."

The Program for International Assessment of Adult Competencies (Piaac) is a test administered to 16 to 65 year-olds in 24 developed countries. It tests three areas: literacy, numeracy, and digital problem-solving.

In a 2016 article in Quartz by Jenny Anderson, reports on the latest survey results.

"In literacy, US adults do okay: the average score across all 24 countries was 273, and the average US adult clocked in at 272, coming in 13th place. In numeracy, things were bleaker: US adults scored 257, significantly below the average of 269, putting them behind Cyprus, Poland, Estonia and the Slovak Republic for an 18th place finish.

"In math, Americans with a high school diploma performed about the same as high school dropouts in other countries.

"In digital problem-solving, US adults came dead last, with a score of 274 compared with an average of 283.

"What's worse, the US has a larger share of low performers in every single area.

Nearly 70% of young adults in the US—aged 16 to 34—either did not finish school or have only a high-school diploma. The average in other countries is 73%, but a larger share of this group in the US scored at the bottom levels of proficiency in reading, math, and digital problem-solving than their international peers.

"Proficiency is defined by breaking down performance into six levels. Countries want lots of people performing at high levels and not so many testing at the bottom levels. For the US, that is not the case. In literacy, Americans have a larger percentage of young adults performing at both the top, which is good, but also at the bottom, which is bad. In math, it's worse: the US has fewer excelling at the top, and more falling in the lower levels."

One of the problems in education today, at least in the US, is that the emphasis is on the curriculum not the student. While recognizing that there needs to be some general principles, this can't be fossilized into one way of teaching. There are many aspects to effective learning, and a standardized curriculum is not one of them. A standardized curriculum and teaching method may have value in being able to assess and compare students, but it is not the best way of teaching, which has to take into account individual talents, brain function and interests.

When I was in clinical practice, I asked virtually all of my student aged "clients" – from those in first grade to college – what their favorite subject was. The majority gave the same answer, but it was not a subject. What was it? (And, no, it wasn't recess).

I asked this question to a small group of experts while participating at a think tank at Yale's School of Education. The experts couldn't get it either.

So, what's the answer?

"The class taught by my favorite teacher."

Learning occurs in the context and service of a relationship.

And moreover, learning occurs when the subject has meaning to the student.

I once had a parent tell me, "My kid is only interested in basketball. Doesn't care for school."

That's because school hasn't been organized from the student's perspective.

Using basketball metaphors and references, I, and I am sure many others, could teach about history, geography, math, science, language, sociology, psychology, pretty much everything.

Unfortunately, conventional education also has its roots in the importance of verbal skills and memorization, which is a disservice to those whose talents lay elsewhere. And the way public education is structured, there isn't the emphasis on finding the student's meaning and interests and using those as vehicles for learning.

All the neuroscience research suggests that active involvement in learning rather than passive receipt of facts, is far more effective. So is physical activity, but that was de-emphasized in public education some time ago. Aerobically fit kids are generally the smartest. In fact, there is a great study conducted by the Napierville, Illinois, USA, school district.

In the 1990s and beyond, the Napierville, Illinois, school district was very proactive in looking for ways to enhance learning. They instituted physical activity programs for their students. However, this wasn't just exercise, it was a range of activities that *matched the children's interests*. So, there were the usual exercise options but also dancing, skipping rope, and so on.

The result of this physical activity was quite amazing. Children who were struggling with their reading and exercised as above, progressed twice as rapidly as their counterparts who had no such physical activity. In another study, exercisers improved their performance 20.4% compared to the non-exercisers, who increased theirs by 3.8%.

More significantly perhaps, the school board entered the entire district as a country in the international tests of math and science, TIMSS. Typically, the USA comes in behind Asian countries on this test, usually about 12th. However, when the Napierville schools entered the TIMSS test they came out number one in the world in Science, narrowly beating out Singapore. Harvard psychiatrist John Ratey writes eloquently about this in his book *Spark.*

Sure, there can be other explanations for these data, but it should be noted that nearly all of the Napierville school children participated in the test not just a select few. Besides, the result is in keeping with what we know about neuroscience; that physical activity increases the neurotransmitters that are helpful in learning. Human beings, especially children, were made to move.

Wherever possible, education needs to be restructured in accordance with what we know about learning. It needs to be taught in the context of a great relationship, made hands-on for better and more realistic engagement, include physical activity and be customized to the student's strengths and interests.

Moreover, in the education space there is the whole topic of college attendance, tuition and relevance. Of course, institutions engage in self-promoting narratives. They promote the notion that college education is essential for life and for future employment. It provides fundamental education and skills in formative years. College graduates will earn more and so on.

However, college debt has risen to an astounding $1.5 trillion, with 44 million people on the hook. Trying to pay off massive debt is likely to influence career choices, not to mention increase stress and anxiety in young people starting out in the careers.

Does college education really need to be 4 years? I got my degree in the UK in three years, because I didn't have to take irrelevant electives like line dancing. And given technological advances, why do you have to attend a lecture in a physical building when you can watch it online? This is an outdated model that is like still using Blockbuster to sell video rather than Netflix. The problem is that can we expect institutions to evolve when they see that as a self-destructive step towards annihilation?

For an in-depth discussion on the issues of institutional stagnation you are encouraged to listed to this great podcast, a dynamic conversation between Peter Thiel and Eric Weinstein.
https://open.spotify.com/episode/732wSQDBZnIqZ0J63nYFsk

Journalism
And finally, to journalism and fake news.

If you have followed along so far, you will have learned that the truth is an ever unfolding commodity. It is almost impossible for a writer on a tight deadline to cover all the relevant facts about an event, certainly the first go round, if ever. Almost by definition, an initial piece of news is likely to be devoid of some critical information. Hopefully, the unfolding information gets covered as the story is updated but that often doesn't happen as the story loses appeal and fades from view.

A second, more slanted view comes when a reporter only writes about the evidence or opinion from one group. For example, an outsider group holds a street demonstration and the reporter only asks members of the group about the value of the event, without getting opinions from others who are not part of the demonstration.

Third, there are many publications pushing an agenda and thus their news will be very slanted and in no way objective.

These publications often use the *false association* method mentioned earlier, pairing two events or ideas that aren't related but making it seem like they are causally connected. They also use emotional anchoring by writing the story in such a way that it arouses emotions in keeping with its agenda.

Then there is outright fake news, where stories are effectively lies masquerading as the truth. The purpose here is to simply spread propaganda which appeals to a certain section of the public. This sells subscriptions but perhaps more importantly leeches into the culture and influences opinions. It is way more toxic and nefarious than we even imagine. As we have seen, people aren't rational independent actors, they are heavily shaped and influenced by the culture.

And here's more disturbing news about fake news.

There are social media groups specifically looking to influence opinion. These could be anything from malicious agencies from foreign governments to misguided hate groups. Numerous viral social media posts with hundreds of thousands or millions of views have been shown to be the work of foreign agents trying, and succeeding, to sow discord. I'm not talking about posts of magnificent animals or adorable children, I'm talking about controversial posts on divisive subjects. When you see those posts, you might do well to assume that you are being manipulated by one rogue group or another which is trying to divide the country.

When you see a controversial social media post, there are some things that you can do to check authenticity.

1. Check the date on any shared videos, photos and texts. These are often from the past, and sometimes years old, but serve the agenda of the group and are made to sound and look current for effect.
2. Try to find out more about the source of the post. Does it come from a specific group, or only shared by people with the same political views?
3. Look at the thread and see the nature of the exchanges. If they are mostly hostile and bigoted, red flags should go up.
4. If any research or data is mentioned, is it publicly available? If so, check the source and see whether the data has been reported accurately. If possible, determine whether the data has been interpreted accurately.

5. Consider the motivation of the people making the post. What might they be trying to do?

Researchers, including cognitive researcher Elizabeth Loftus mentioned earlier, conducted a study on fake news just prior to the Irish 2018 referendum on the legalization of abortion.

More than 3000 voters were contacted online and asked how they would vote in the referendum. Subjects were then presented with six news reports which included two fake reports. These reports reflected inflammatory behavior by a person on each side of the proposition.

The subjects were subsequently asked about whether they had heard about these events and whether they had specific memories of them. Then the subjects were told that two of the six stories were fake and asked them to identify which ones they were.

Almost half of the subjects then reported a memory for one of the fake events. Subjects were more likely to recall memories of inflammatory fake events *that opposed* their own position. So pro-abortion voters were more likely to recall anti-abortion inflammatory behavior, while anti-abortion voters were more likely to recall pro-abortion inflammatory behavior.

"This demonstrates the ease with which we can plant these entirely fabricated memories, despite this voter suspicion and even despite an explicit warning that they may have been shown fake news," says Gillian Murphy, of the University of College Cork and lead author of the study.

"In highly emotional, partisan political contests, such as the 2020 US Presidential election, voters may 'remember' entirely fabricated news stories. In particular, they are likely to 'remember' scandals that reflect poorly on the opposing candidate," added Murphy.

This example *of confirmation bias* shows how pervasive fake news can be. Given the power it has to create false narratives and memories one has to consider this nothing less than brainwashing at quite a high level.

https://journals.sagepub.com/doi/abs/10.1177/0956797619864887?journalCode=pssa

If we are concerned about Free Hearing as much as we are about Free Speech, it's important to understand these various techniques and our susceptibility to manipulation. The human mind is easily manipulated and if you don't want to become a pawn in someone else's game, it's important to take steps to limit your vulnerability.

It is now relatively easy for any agency to influence social discourse, create divide, and sow and grow the seeds of discontent. This is a major problem that involves educating people and developing some safeguards against the misuse of technology.

In 2014 Finland launched an anti-fake news initiative that has been getting recognition from other countries. The education program involves getting people to think critically about what they are viewing and sharing, as well as ways of identifying fake news.

In an article on the CNN website, Jussi Toivanen, the Finnish chief communications specialist for the prime minister's office, said "it is difficult to pinpoint the exact number of misinformation operations to have targeted the country in recent years, but most play on issues like immigration, the European Union, or whether Finland should become a full member of NATO (Russia is not a fan)."

Toivanen is quoted as saying that "It's not just a government problem, the whole society has been targeted. We are doing our part, but it's everyone's task to protect the Finnish democracy. The first line of defense is the kindergarten teacher."

The program has focused on providing children and teenagers tools for spotting misinformation.

As Eliza Mackintosh wrote in her CNN piece, https://edition.cnn.com/interactive/2019/05/europe/finland-fake-news-intl/

"The exercises include examining claims found in YouTube videos and social media posts, comparing media bias in an array of different "clickbait" articles, probing how misinformation preys on readers' emotions, and even getting students to try their hand at writing fake news stories themselves."

With technology now able to completely simulate realistic but totally fake videos in which anyone can be made to appear to endorse anything, there will be a need to spread this education as well as tech safeguards that will minimize the threat of total chaos that could be perpetrated by anyone, from a small group of tech guys, to an organized hate group, to the governments of hostile forces.

Institutional Change
Some of the above examples involve institutions. If it's difficult for people to change, it's even more difficult for institutions to transform. They are totally invested in the status quo and any significant change is threatening. This is the challenge: how does an institution change in a way that is not self-destructive?   That ever-present fear of self-destruction then engages all the cognitive biases which then justify no real change at all.

Of course, it's all about the money. If, for example, higher education changed to where there was really no justification or need for students to actually be on a campus, the whole financial structure of higher education institutions would dramatically change, and revenues shrink dramatically.

If ultimately what creates change is economics, then it might just be you have more power at the check-out counter then the ballot box. I never want to discourage people from voting, but realize that when you buy something you are supporting the institution or entity that is selling it.

Relationships

Our relationships are perhaps our most important assets. Given the complexity and the almost inevitable errors in our thinking it's amazing that any two people can get along. There's so much room for misinterpretation that it is truly staggering that friendships and more intimate relationships can endure. However, there's a thinking error in that statement.

Cognitive bias can just as easily have a positive impact as a negative impact on a relationship. Consider, for example, the Halo effect, or even the love virus example given earlier. And if you're emotionally invested in anything, you'll work hard to see it in a positive light. And conversely, if you're angry enough, you can give up anything, including your marriage. That, incidentally, was a tactic that I often used when trying to help people quit addictive habits.

When people came to see me, for example, to quit smoking, my first question would be something to the effect of...

"Why the hell do you want to quit?"

I knew that simply going on and on about the dangers of smoking, would bore the man to death and maybe even put up his defenses. He had heard all that before and he still hadn't quit. Besides, I wanted to hear his motivation, not mine.

While it was nice to talk about all the health advantages and financial benefits of quitting, if I could link quitting to a strong existing emotion, I knew there was a much greater chance of success. I had to find the emotion that was already there in his brain and activate it.

One tactic I used a couple of times, revolved around my client's political beliefs, because they tend to have emotional value and significance. This happened to coincide with a time when the Labour party was strong in the UK and even formed governments on occasion.

If my client was avidly socialist, I could casually drop into conversation, almost as an off-hand comment, that "those capitalist tobacco companies have really got you by the b****."

It worked! Faced with the inconsistency of beliefs, something needed to give, and often it was the cigarettes that went up in smoke. (For more about communication strategies that actually influence people please see my book *Power Talk; The Art of Effective Communication*).

Communication can be very problematic because of the parties' own biases and perceptions.

Two of my favorite authors are Sigmund Freud and Dave Barry, the humor writer.

I find Freud very amusing and have gained great psychological insights from Dave Barry.

Now, Freud obviously had a massive effect of culture as described in the defense mechanisms chapters, and had great insight into the human condition. For example, one of my favorite insightful Freud quotes is:

"Time spent with cats is never wasted."

One of my favorite Dave Barry examples comes from his excellent book *Dave Barry's Guide to Guys* an enlightening insight into gender differences, communication and thinking.

In one of the stories in this book, Barry writes about a couple, Elaine and Roger, who are in the car together. Elaine asks Roger as they are driving back from a night out, whether he realizes that it is exactly six months since they started dating.

There is a loud silence, which has Elaine wondering whether Roger wants more space in the relationship, and she begins to chide herself for bringing the subject up. Then she reflects on whether she herself is indeed ready for a committed relationship, children and the white picket fence. As Dave Barry describes it…

"Roger is actually thinking six months…So that means it was… let's see…February when we starting going out, which was right after I had the car at the dealer's…which means…let me check the odometer…whoa, I'm way overdue for an oil change here!

"And Elaine is thinking: he's upset. I can see it on his face. Maybe I'm reading this completely wrong. Maybe he wants *more* from our relationship, *more* intimacy, *more* commitment. Maybe he has sensed – even before *I* sensed it – that I was feeling some reservations. Yes, I bet that's it. That's why he is reluctant to say anything about his own feelings. He is afraid of being rejected."

"And Roger is thinking: And I'm gonna have them look at the transmission again. I don't care what those morons say, it's still not shifting right. And they better not try to blame it on the cold weather this time. What cold weather, its eighty-seven degrees out and this thing is shifting like a goddam garbage truck and I paid those incompetent thieving cretin bastards *six hundred dollars.*

"And Elaine is thinking: He's angry. And I don't blame him. I'd be angry too. God, I feel so guilty putting him through this, but I can't help the way I feel. I'm not sure."

"And Roger is thinking: They'll probably say it's only a ninety-day warranty. That's exactly what they are going to say, the scumballs."

"And Elaine is thinking: Maybe I'm just too idealistic, waiting for a knight to come riding up in his white horse, when I'm sitting next to a perfectly good person, a person I enjoy being with, a person I truly do care about, a person who seems to truly care about me. A person who is in pain because of my self-centered schoolgirl romantic fantasy."

"And Roger is thinking: Warranty? They want a warranty? I'll give them a goddamn warranty. I'll take their warranty and stick it up their..."

"Please don't torture yourself like this," Elaine says, her eyes beginning to brim with tears. "Maybe I should never have.... Oh God I feel so... *(she breaks down sobbing)*.

"What?" says Roger.

"I'm such a fool," Elaine sobs. "I mean I know there's no knight. I really know that. It's silly. There's no knight and there's no horse either."

"There's no horse?" says Roger.

"You think that I'm a damn fool don't you," Elaine says.

"No," says Roger glad to finally know the correct answer.

"It's just that I...It's that I...I need some more time," Elaine says.

"They finally depart and Elaine spends the entire on her bed a conflicted tortured soul and weeps until dawn, whereas Roger gets back to his place, opens a bag of Doritos and turns on the TV and immediately becomes deeply involved in a rerun of a tennis match between two Czechoslavakians he has never heard of."

Later, Roger asks a friend who knows Elaine, an important question.

"Did Elaine ever own a horse?"

> *"The single biggest problem with communication is the illusion that it has taken place." – George Bernard Shaw*

Dave Barry's brilliant example shows how easy it is for us to miscommunicate both other people's, and our own perceptions, and feelings. And as the example shows, the escalating narratives only serve to take us further and further from the truth.

This is what happens during an argument. Emotion runs high, bias intervenes and before too long, a couple that just a few hours before were getting along great, are now headed for divorce.

An argument starts and the anger ramps up. In this state, the default position is now to verbalize all the things about your partner that make you angry. This leads to an *availability cascade* where your mind fills with only negative examples of your partner's behavior. This then distorts the narrative and *anchors* you to a very negative perception where only the worst aspects of your partner's behavior are recalled.

In all likelihood your partner is doing the same and before long the available and predominant perception of both parties is that the relationship sucks. At which point, one or both parties embraces the notion of a divorce, which clouds perception even more. It can also lead to the *optimism bias* or fantasy of how another relationship would be perfectly awesome, and before long both parties are convinced that the other person is satanic and needs to be ejected from their lives. This then becomes the narrative all the way through the divorce proceedings, with the perception hardening with each hearing.

And here's something even more disturbing.

Even if you are subsequently convinced that your narrative was completely off target, it still remains there in your mind, waiting to be activated on a triggering perception. As they say, you never get a second chance to make a first impression. An impression hangs around with impressive persistence. Once an image or even an idea is put in your brain, there it stays. You never get a chance to get rid of any impression. Which is, of course, why false accusations, whether they are believed by the accuser or not, are so damning. And so is fake news.

This dynamic and subsequent bias can and will influence you for years, if not forever if you let it. It will certainly influence your choice of people for all sorts of different relationships.

When you have had a "negative" experience in a relationship, it will bias you whole perception. Remember, we overvalue fear. So, you have built up an overexaggerated fear and bias about certain aspects of your ex's behavior. Which means that what you then do will be...

to overestimate a particularly negative characteristic, and that will dominate and anchor your thoughts and subsequent choices about relationships.

There was a media piece going around some time ago about a man who divorced his wife. His main complaint was that his ex-wife, simply dominated conversations, and went on and on and on and on and on.

He subsequently married a woman who was mute!

Perhaps that's an extreme example, but a good one nonetheless that speaks to the questioning of anchoring, or the *focalism bias* in which one thought totally dominates, and fundamentally distorts, the narrative.

Questions
1. What were your favorite classes in school?
2. When you're emotional are you able to manage your thoughts so they don't get out of hand?
3. What are your cognitive strengths (e.g. verbal memory, visual-spatial skills)?
4. If you were to optimally structure learning for yourself what would it look like?

Chapter Fifteen

Science and Pseudoscience

Assuming that scientists must be ultra-rational people because of what they do, is a leap of faith. Scientists are human and so just as subject to the same thinking fallibilities as everyone else. Some of these fallibilities manifest in their science work. For example, there are standard statistical tests that determine whether differences between groups on a particular variable are significant or not. It is not uncommon for authors of scientific papers to say something to the effect that "although the results didn't reach statistical significance, there was a trend towards it" and then use that as basis for justifying a particular theory. There is no trend towards significance. The test is either significant or it isn't. That's like a soccer team who have tied a game 1-1 declaring themselves the winner on the grounds that "we almost scored a few times".

However, what follows does not invalidate scientific enquiry. Far from it. It merely warns of the human biases that can disrupt the process. Scientific enquiry is still the best model we have for trying to think rationally and with awareness of what is not known. When practiced ethically and honestly, it is the best way of digging deep into what is happening and to understand the myriad of factors that influence any process under investigation. So, please don't resort to binary thinking and use what is mentioned below as a way of discrediting science. These are just factors that will help you be discerning in your analysis of information presented as scientific findings.

Types of Scientific Research

Cross-sectional: A group of people is assessed on various measures at just *one point* in time. Limited value, and certainly can't be used to prove anything.

Longitudinal: A series of assessments on various measures are repeated on the same subject over a period of time. Definitely can show the impact of an intervention, although can only hint at cause and needs literally thousands of subjects to be valuable.

Meta Analyses: A series of many research papers are reviewed and summarized. Useful for looking at overall trends in the field and the replication of ideas. However, limited because it doesn't have access to negative results, which typically aren't published.

Interventional double blind case control studies: This is the pinnacle of research, in which two similar groups are studied. One group receives an intervention and the other receives a placebo or no intervention. Both groups are followed over a period of time. If there is a significant difference between the two groups, it is reasonable to assume that the treatment had an effect.

Science and Pseudoscience

In today's world of social media, TED talks and book contracts, the name of the game for an academic is to develop a theory, lay claim to it (often by giving at fancy name) and monetize it. This leads to several trends in science.

The first is "research" which simply has too few cases to make any meaningful conclusions. Really effective research requires literally thousands of subjects and that is difficult and expensive and very few studies have the power to make meaningful conclusions.

Second, science, especially behavioral science, depends on replications of research to validate and fine tune findings. But who wants to replicate other people's research ideas? Most researchers want to follow their own ideas. As a result, there are not enough replication studies. As a guide, the introduction section of a research paper helps guide you as to its value. Does it reference many other studies tackling the same topic, showing this is part of a serious scientific effort, or are there only a few references to similar research?

Third, almost all behavioral research generates correlations, which are not indication of causality. Even a positive correlation is difficult to interpret. In the 1980s there was a strong correlation between VCR sales and HIV diagnoses. One year in Norway there was a good correlation between the number of storks that were seen and recorded births. A reputable scientist, especially in behavioral and health research, will point out that an association doesn't mean a causal relationship.

For example, a study shows that people who live near major highways have poorer health. Is that because of the toxins they inhale from the traffic? Is that because the noise keeps them awake and disrupts their sleep? Or is it because homes near highways are typically cheaper and residents here have a lower SES which is associated with poorer health in general? Or is it a combination of some of these factors influencing each other. Or is the association due to some yet unconsidered factors? You can see why research is peeling the layers back of a very large onion and can only be revealed over time with many studies involving literally thousands of people.

Fourth, most people don't want to publish insignificant results, so there's a bias towards the publication of research which seems to show a positive effect. In the original Prozac research, 94% of successful trials were published whereas only 51% of the unsuccessful ones were. And incidentally, negative results are far less likely to be mentioned by other researchers, reducing their influence yet further.

Fifth, there are numerous ways of fudging data. These include finding a statistical test that gives you the result you want, omitting some contrary data because...well, they mess up the findings, and omitting to mention "negative results." One variation on this latter option is to test hundreds of variables because there is then the excellent probability *simply by chance* that you will find one that generates a significant result. You then triumphantly report that significant result and neglect to mention the other 300 variables that showed absolutely no significant differences whatsoever.

Sixth, and perhaps more importantly, the way science has been conducted, there is a serious danger that it inadvertently, or advertently, leads to key misperceptions.

Let's look at neuroscience research. The advent of technology has allowed us some insights into the brain. We can see, for example, which areas of the brain are stimulated in certain cognitive activities, the structure of the brain, and so on. However, the way that most research is constructed it can only look at a small number of variables and *address co-occurrence and association but not causality*. And although many scientists will preface their comments about the lack of causal direction or causality at all in their findings, this often gets lost on the public, and even within the scientific community.

For example, an autopsy reveals that a woman who had a lot of stress in the last decade of her life shows an abnormal brain structure. The *false association* tendency will lead most to believe that her abnormal brain structure was responsible for stress. The problems with this conclusion, apart from it being a single case study which has very limited, if any, value, are:

1. Without a pre-stress brain scan, there's no sure way of knowing what her brain looked like *before* the stress. There have been several cases of people who lead seemingly normal lives and have even achieved a lot, who had brain autopsies that showed serious structural abnormalities.
2. The relation of a brain scan to stress is also determined by what variables the researchers chose to investigate. Perhaps there was also a correlation between her structural brain abnormality and the time she spent watching TV or the amount of pizza she ate.
3. Even if there is indeed a connection between chronic stress and brain structure, the natural question is what is the direction of the effect; does the brain create the stress, or the stress create the brain structure? However, that is NOT the question. That is another example of binary thinking.

   The question is how does stress influence brain structure and how does brain structure influence stress? And what's the nature of any likely reciprocal relationship?

(Another issue is the total acceptance of the infallibility of technology. FMRI machines need to be configured depending on the type of scan and in one study, less than perfect configuration led to research that revealed that dead salmon showed brain responses to pictures of human beings. Very fishy!)

This, of course, increases the magnitude and complexity (and cost) of the research.

This isn't insignificant and just a philosophical exercise.

If the assumption is that the brain is responsible for everything in a deterministic way, then all attempts to change behavior or treat health issues, will be seen through the lens of the brain. So, if you are depressed, you must have some brain dysfunction that needs to be treated with medication, despite the fact that there is very little evidence that a brain dysfunction causes depression.

The notion that your brain is the computer that runs everything and must therefore be the cause of all mental and cognitive issues is way too simplistic. The computer analogy is acceptable **if** you understand that a computer's output is a not just a product of its functioning *but also how its programmed.*

We know that the brain, above all, is a very trainable organ. It learns from your input more than anything else. There's a reciprocal relationship between you -- all aspects of you from your physiology to behavior to thoughts and emotions – and brain output and even structure. We know that our actions actually can change the structure and function of the brain.

The brain, therefore, is not a fixed and rigid machine, it *adapts* to your experience. And it *influences* your experience.   And your experience, which is influenced by the brain, *influences the brain.*

Consequently, a medication for a psychiatric condition might attenuate how a patient feels, but might not do much to change the process underlying the condition. For example, a medication to reduce anxiety, might make you feel less anxious, but might do nothing to change your experience-brain interaction that drives the anxiety process.

As you can tell, this non-binary conception makes life and research way more complex and difficult. However, that doesn't mean it's wrong. It just means that results need to be "interpreted with caution" and have to be replicated by other independent research groups. And it's always the case that "more research is needed."

The fact is that human beings reflect nature. And everywhere we see that nature works through interconnection and reciprocal relationships that defy a simply deterministic approach to understanding.

Interdependence is essential.

For more about the irrationality of scientific research the reader is directed to the "9 Circles of Scientific Hell" which can be found here:

http://blogs.discovermagazine.com/neuroskeptic/2010/11/24/the-9-circles-of-scientific-hell/#.V45tgTceXNV

There are several things that can distinguish real science from pseudoscience. Here are some ways to test the distinction.

1. Look at the source of the research. Is it independent or funded by an organization with a vested interest? Money talks and influences scientific results.
2. What is the agenda and the context of the article? Is it introducing a brand new discovery, typically a "cure" for something that many people suffer from but have so far been unaware of? Or is a "miracle" cure?
3. Does the article use testimonials instead of scientific objective data?
4. Does the article make it sound like this is a revolutionary breakthrough?
5. Are there lots of exclamations marks, questions and much, much more!
6. Does it imply that this new technique, or whatever, is exclusive? Exclusivity is not the hallmark of serious science that has been building over many years.
7. Is there a story involved about how one person followed their instincts and discovered something completely new?

In addition to these considerations, even when scientific research is conducted and interpreted accurately, there is the serious danger that the media and public will misinterpret it.

Perhaps you have heard that 93% of all communication is non-verbal. Words don't mean much? Scrap all those quotes and replace them with gestures? Well, not so fast.

Albert Mehrabian conducted research in which a person said a few *words that reflected emotion* and had subjects guess the intent of the communication. In the study there was also a conflict between the words spoken and non-verbal behavior displayed. Under these circumstances, 93% of the subjects' judgments were based on non-verbal aspects of the communication. Hardly surprising, when only a few words were uttered in an unnatural context that really didn't reflect what people would consider a normal interaction. Well, it wasn't even an interaction. Oh, and the results only apply to women because there were no male subjects used.

So, if you're having a one way conversation in which there are few words spoken, and those that are spoken are designed to elicit emotion, and there is conflict between the spoken word and non-verbal behavior, chances are good that most interpretation will be based on non-verbal cues, at least for women. The generalization of that finding to normal interaction is obviously flawed and absurd. I used to quote this statistic myself because I was too lazy to consult the original research, but when I did, I realized my mistake.

The scientific process of gathering data and objectively analyzing it while controlling as many of the variables as possible is indeed an essential part of critical thinking. But let's not make the mistake of thinking that all science therefore is objective and free of the usual biases inherent in human thinking. Some of the time it isn't.

You can't measure, much less control, much less know all the relevant variables. Moreover, science is an evolving process. What we believe to be true today will be expanded upon, discounted and even disproved in the next few decades or less. It's always a work in progress.

To make matters worse, scientific "facts" are then not only inaccurately characterized in the popular media, they are often hijacked and used to manipulate people. Freud in particular was very concerned that psychiatric ideas and insights about how the mind works, would indeed be hijacked by marketers to manipulate people. Ironically it was one of his family members who did just that on global scale.

The BBC produced a great documentary called the *Century of the Self,* which highlights this very process. Writing about it in the British newspaper The Guardian in 2002, Tim Adams wrote: (https://www.theguardian.com/education/2002/mar/10/medicalscience.highereducation)

"Sigmund Freud may have invented the Self, full of unspoken dreams and desires, but it was his American nephew, Edward Bernays, who packaged it and put it on to the market. Suddenly, everyone wanted one. And, of course, no one wanted one that was quite the same as anyone else's."

"Bernays, was born in Vienna in 1891, and had worked in his late twenties as a propagandist for America, a role he continued in after the war. Being aware of psychological influence, he invented a brand new name for his line of work: public relations. Bernays' influence continued for a long time as he lived to be 103. His clients included Presidents Coolidge, Wilson, Hoover and Eisenhower, as well as Thomas Edison, Caruso, Nijinsky, and scores of the largest corporations and many foreign governments. But his greatest "success" was selling his uncle Sigmund's ideas of the wild and untamed subconscious to the American public and to American business."

"Bernays popularized his uncle's ideas by finding publishers for them and propagandizing them in the United States. Like his uncle, he believed that man was controlled by his irrational desires and that by applying psychoanalytic principles, these desires could be harnessed and used on a large scale, for power and profit. Thus, the hijacking of psychological principles, or what were seen as psychological principles, had begun on a massive scale."

As Adam writes:
"Bernays was among the first to understand that one of the implications of the subconscious mind was that it could be appealed to in order to sell products and ideas. You no longer had to offer people what they needed; by linking your brand with their deeper hopes and fears, you could persuade them to buy what they dreamt of. Equipped with our subconscious wish-lists, we could go shopping for the life we had seen portrayed in the adverts.

"You didn't buy a new car because the old one had burnt out; you bought a more modern one to increase your self-esteem, or a more low-slung one to enhance your sense of your sex-appeal. You didn't choose a pair of running shoes for comfort or practicality; you did so because somewhere deep inside you, you felt they might liberate you to 'Just Do It'. And you didn't vote for a political party out of duty, or because you believed it had the best policies to advance the common good; you did so because of a secret feeling that it offered you the most likely opportunity to promote and express your Self. 'Our people,' said Herbert Hoover, 'have been transformed into constantly moving happiness machines.'"

In this way, Western society has made the feelings and desires of the individual sacred.

The fact that science has been hijacked in this way, isn't the fault of science. Scientific methods are still the best tools to help us minimize our cognitive biases and appreciate and develop logical analysis. Unfortunately, the way they are presented in educational settings doesn't do justice to their importance in everyday life. Physics, for example, isn't just about atoms and quarks, it is about uncertainty and the beauty and perils of determinism. Call it physics if you want but it can also be valuable in training your mind about money, relationships, careers, -- everything.

The Scientific method isn't just about science, it's *critical thinking about anything*. It is about the methods of logic and rationality and how to identify bias and distortion.

Chapter Sixteen

Culture and Philosophy

As we have seen, one of the biggest influences on our thinking, perception and emotional expression is our culture. One can see major differences in the roots of Western and Eastern thought for example, that will significantly impact the thinking process. Fortunately, the massive increase in communication has allowed some people to integrate the best of both traditions but there are still major implicit messages in different cultures.

Eastern tradition is based on the acceptance, reverence and cooperation with nature. For example, Eastern medical traditions are focused on using natural remedies, and leading people back to a natural wholeness. Eastern cultures are also socio-centric, with a focus on interdependence and connectivity. Moreover, eastern tradition focuses on experiences not just behaviors. It recognizes something more than just scientific probabilities.

Western tradition, especially since the Reformation and the rise of science, has been focused on rationality, with a focus on behavior rather than experience. The West is also largely an egocentric culture that focuses on the individual's potential and independence rather than interdependence. The West also is in competition with nature, trying to use and dominate it. For example, it uses synthesized drugs to cure people of symptoms and focuses on illness rather than health and wellness.

In other critical ways, the East values perfect balance, the West values perfection.

An over-emphasis on the individual actually harms the individual. It gives a false sense of importance and entitlement. By valuing independence, it can minimize interdependence, and however you look it at you have to conclude that at some level, interdependence is a reality and a necessity. You may be worth billions of dollars and can buy whatever you like at the store, but someone has to make the product, ship the product, store the product and sell you the product. We don't live in a social vacuum.

As I wrote in my book *Power Talk*:

"No Man is an island and those who inspire to be are more Alcatraz than Hilton Head."

Indeed, the study and definition of happiness has evolved to the point where happiness, defined by the word eudemonia (literally "good spirit") entails compassion, virtue, cooperation and interdependence. People often use happiness to mean fleeting pleasure or lack of stress, but that is pleasure and relaxation, not happiness. As Eleanor Roosevelt said:

"Happiness is not a goal, it is a by-product. Paradoxically, the one sure way not to be happy is deliberately to map out a way of life in which one would please oneself completely and exclusively. For what keeps our interest in life and makes us look forward to tomorrow is giving pleasure to other people."

Studies of eudemonia around the world typically find that eudemonia does not come from possessions or wealth. Certainly, financial stress is real and suffered by many, but relieving that stress is relief, not happiness. It is estimated that over the equivalent of an annual income of about $70,000 in the US, wealth doesn't add to happiness. Surely you have heard about all those miserable, sometimes bankrupt, sometimes even suicidal lottery winners? Are they just poor money managers or have they found out the disappointing reality that money doesn't buy you happiness?

The cultural messaging in the western world then is that happiness can be pursued, and wealth will provide happiness, both of which are questionable ideas at best and plainly false at worst.

In addition, western cultural messaging suggests that one can become anything we want, that we are awesome, and that if we master a few key behaviors we will be a success, find wealth and happiness, be fully independent and contribute to society, possibly by curing cancer or solving the Middle East problem. We are defined by independent outcomes.

The conventional view of the wise man in the eastern tradition is quite different. It is much more defined by internal measures of who you are, rather than external measures of how much you have, which is why the sages of virtually all traditions had NO possessions. In this tradition, virtue is as important as skill, and compassion, connection and interdependency are measures of wisdom and eudemonia. In this tradition, there is much more virtue and value in a life of struggle, adaptation, persistence and development, than external "success." Such a life only helps the person to grow significantly and that growth is what is valuable to self and others, indeed contributes to the evolution of the human race, and leads to eudemonia.

Frederich Nietzsche followed this tradition with his 'ubermensch,' a sort of superman who evolved beyond current human status and much more towards, and possibly beyond, a concept of God. The fact that Nietsche, the son of a preacher, famously said that 'God is Dead' reflects the fact as humans evolve they are likely to discard older concepts of universality and replace them with new more relativistic definitions. So, through evolution, God as currently conceived would change into a different concept; we can't say what that concept will be because we're not there yet.

Parenthetically, some of Nietzsche's work is associated with fascism but that was because after his death, his sister, a Nazi sympathizer used it to justify her political beliefs. This has led to misunderstandings about Nietzsche's work and philosophy.

The ubermensch was destined to sacrifice and suffer for the sake of human evolution, and more specifically, the next generation. Nietzsche's view of a meaningful and eudemonious life looks like this:

"The most intelligent men, like the strongest, find their happiness where others would find only disaster: in the labyrinth, in being hard with themselves and with others, in effort; their delight is self-mastery; in them asceticism becomes second nature, a necessity, as instinct."

A key then to both wisdom and eudemonia, is to recognize the traditions from which concepts are based, and to question their validity, reliability and applicability.

For example, the western tradition focuses on behaviors and skills. This is often stressed to the point of absurdity.

The Five Steps to Climbing Mt Everest.
1. Buy some mountaineering gear
2. Firm up travel plans to Nepal
3. Select a Sherpa to help you
4. Go to base camp
5. Start Climbing

The fact is that while the skills and behaviors are important what is also key is your experience while doing them. Your purpose is also critical; why do you want to climb Everest in the first place?

The role of meaning and purpose is so critical in every sphere of human activity. Can you believe it took corporations, leaders and entrepreneurs until the 21st century to realize, or accept, that workers and employees need to be engaged in their work to be really productive. Duh!

Cultural beliefs and traditions, shape even the approach and response to medical treatment. Mario Martinez is a clinical neuropsychologist who has developed a bio-cognitive theory that argues that physical responses are bio-social and cultural. For example, in writing about aging, Martinez writes:

"I argue that growing older is the cognitive and biological accumulation of time, whereas aging is the consequences of our behavior contextualized within a cultural history. In other words, the passing of time is necessary but not sufficient to account for the cognitive and biological changes that transpire in the aging process. A culture defines the biocultural portals as well as interprets the health and the quality of aging. The biocultural portals are defined by the scientific, aesthetic and transcendental beliefs that are assimilated by the culture. For example, while a 62 year old from an industrialized culture is engaged in behaviors conducive to achieving retirement, a Tarahumara Indian counterpart of the Chihuahua region of Mexico may be running up to 200 miles in a competitive racing sport called "kick ball" that can last several days (Pelletier, 1981). The Tarahumaras, known for their longevity, believe that growing older makes them stronger and consequently better runners. Retirement is not one of their biocultural portals. Interestingly, since the Tarahumaras look forward to their expected physical gains from growing older, "middle age crisis" is unknown and the usual degenerative pathology associated with aging is rare in their culture."[13]

We need to understand the fundamental assumptions that drive our biases and our thinking.

---

[13] Martinez, M; (2003). A Biocultural Model of Aging.
The International Journal of Systems and Cybernetics 32 (5/6), 653-657.

Is there really such a thing as an overnight success? How is success defined?

Are setbacks really disasters or are they the best learning and development opportunities?

Is the American Dream a constructed fantasy perpetuated by the relatively small numbers who seemed to have found it?

What is the role of pleasure as opposed to eudemonia in our lives?

Is a life of continual pleasure, really meaningful or just one long yawn and abandonment of principle? I mean have you ever seen happy protesters? Don't you need a degree of angst or even anger to fight injustice? Or do you just turn a blind eye to unfairness and pretend everything is wonderful?

These are important issues which impact your direction in life, and your evaluation of yourself. And they are affected by cultural messaging that can and does influence your thinking.

Words that describe the thought process
Stoop-id-ity; from Stoop: to lower, and id: basic instincts. i.e. to lower oneself to basic instincts. To give in to your lower power.

Simpl-idiocy: To deal in simplistic, artificial divisions and thus fail to recognize complexity

Problem-otion: The excessive influence of emotion on thought

Chapter Seventeen

The Future of Mankind

The advent of social media has given a voice to almost everybody on the planet. And when most of us are story-tellers driven by emotional comfort, this has not helped in the development, or maintenance, of rational discourse. Instead, we have opinions masquerading as facts and emotional outbursts.

Being offended is not a position, it is an emotional expression. In fact, it is an attempt at emotional manipulation. However, that's hardly surprising because, as pointed out in chapter 9, in a marketing culture most forms of communication are emotional manipulation.

"Discussion" has descended into an exhibition of defense mechanisms; mostly psychotic, immature and maladaptive. Adaptive mechanisms suggest an openness and respect of other opinions that isn't apparent much of the time. Debate has been replaced by insult and even slander. It's not the path to greatness but it is good for ratings, votes and sales.

The problem is that this sets the tone of the culture and is the example being set for future generations. Even in places of higher education, which one would hope to be a bastion of rational and respectful discussion, gossip, opinion and political correctness often reign supreme. And serious attempts at self-evaluation are discouraged for fear of showing the cognitive bias that is used to support the status quo.

One of the assumptions that guides this behavior is that if you're not aggressively attacking an opponent, say in a political election, you will be seen either as weak or without any ammunition. I wonder whether that perception is accurate?

I wonder what would happen if a political candidate said in a public discussion forum something to the effect that...

"I respect my opponent. He (or she) tries hard and I am not going to exaggerate false claims or any claims against him. That's not what I do. However, I believe we do have differences on policy and that is what I am committed to."

I guess the answer is that the people who want to see him as weak will do so, the people who want to see him as strong and will do so but what about the remainder? How will they perceive him?

In addition, despite the propagation of the illusion that everyone in the US is equal, in many ways they aren't. There are broadly five parts to the US (and many other countries') caste system:

Very low SES which includes the very poor, the homeless and many who are mentally ill.

Low SES, those who live in or just above poverty and suffer in terms of major indicators like health and education

The Middle Class, who have just about enough money to afford a home and the basics of a western life with occasional pleasures like vacations

The Upper Middle Class, who have more than many and can enjoy expensive goods and live without financial stress

The Ruling Elite who have most of the money and the power.

In this system, everyone is important – or should be. For a society to be really great it needs to ensure that almost everyone has a role in the culture and can contribute to it. This means that the ruling elite are sensitive enough to ensure fairness and rational strategies and decisions about the country. This is key. The British might have been imperialists, but they did try to practice and teach administrative justice, which is perhaps why no British colony (and the Brits once ruled 25% of the earth) has ever turned to communism.

However, one cannot dismiss economics. To service all the sectors of society requires money. If you are married and have three kids, you want to live in comfortable environment, give your family at least adequate if not preferred opportunities for education, travel, etc. However, that requires a lot of money. If you don't have it, you can always borrow, but that could end in a collapsing house of cards. Similarly, with a society, the economy has to be strong to give everyone a chance of finding meaning, contributing and meeting their goals. If the economy isn't strong, and money is tight, you've got problems.

I'm not an economist but experts that I trust believe that the US economy has been stagnant for the best part of the past fifty years. And you can look at countries like Venezuela, where corruption has prevailed and wealth siphoned off by the ruling elite, and see what happens when there is an damagingly unequal redistribution of wealth.

It is true the power corrupts but we have to understand that is a temptation for any of us in such a position. It's easy – and often accurate – to complain that the ruling elite are simply protecting their best interests, but who amongst us wouldn't do the same in that position? This doesn't justify it, but hopefully it focuses our attention on the default position of power and makes us vigilant about protecting the system, which should be our priority, not attacking people for being as biased as we are. We simply have to ensure, and certainly hope, that the power is exercised with compassion and fairness.

But what happens when cognitive bias rather than rationality is the norm? What happens when emotional manipulation is mistaken for rationality? What happens when the different strata of society become so alienated from each other that all they can do is attack each other with invective and hate?

In that case the country will eventually descend into chaos and disaster.

There is much to be learned from history and specifically the collapse of previous civilizations. We will need to think rationally and without cognitive bias to seriously save ourselves from collapse.

Luke Kemp is a researcher based at the Centre for the Study of Existential Risk at the University of Cambridge. He wrote a piece called "Are we on the road to civilization collapse" that appeared on the BBC Future website in February of 2019.
(http://www.bbc.com/future/story/20190218-are-we-on-the-road-to-civilisation-collapse)

In the article Kemp writes:

"Collapse is often quick and greatness provides no immunity. The Roman Empire covered 4.4 million square km (1.9 million square miles) in 390. Five years later, it had plummeted to 2 million square km (770,000 square miles). By 476, the empire's reach was zero."

"Societies of the past and present are just complex systems composed of people and technology. The theory of "normal accidents" suggests that complex technological systems regularly give way to failure. So, collapse may be a normal phenomenon for civilizations, regardless of their size and stage."

"We may be more technologically advanced now. But this gives little ground to believe that we are immune to the threats that undid our ancestors. Our newfound technological abilities even bring new, unprecedented challenges to the mix."

"And while our scale may now be global, collapse appears to happen to both sprawling empires and fledgling kingdoms alike. There is no reason to believe that greater size is armour against societal dissolution. Our tightly-coupled, globalised economic system is, if anything, more likely to make crisis spread."

Kemp then outlines the factors that spur civilization demise writing...

"CLIMATIC CHANGE: When climatic stability changes, the results can be disastrous, resulting in crop failure, starvation and desertification.

"ENVIRONMENTAL DEGRADATION: Collapse can occur when societies overshoot the carrying capacity of their environment. This ecological collapse theory, which has been the subject of bestselling books, points to excessive deforestation, water pollution, soil degradation and the loss of biodiversity as precipitating causes.

"INEQUALITY AND OLIGARCHY: Wealth and political inequality can be central drivers of social disintegration, as can oligarchy and centralisation of power among leaders. This not only causes social distress, but handicaps a society's ability to respond to ecological, social and economic problems.

"COMPLEXITY: Collapse expert and historian Joseph Tainter has proposed that societies eventually collapse under the weight of their own accumulated complexity and bureaucracy. Societies are problem-solving collectives that grow in complexity in order to overcome new issues. However, the returns from complexity eventually reach a point of diminishing returns. After this point, collapse will eventually ensue.

"EXTERNAL SHOCKS: In other words, the "four horsemen": war, natural disasters, famine and plagues. The Aztec Empire, for example, was brought to an end by Spanish invaders. Most early agrarian states were fleeting due to deadly epidemics. The concentration of humans and cattle in walled settlements with poor hygiene made disease outbreaks unavoidable and catastrophic. Sometimes disasters combined, as was the case with the Spanish introducing salmonella to the Americas.

"RANDOMNESS/BAD LUCK: Statistical analysis on empires suggests that collapse is random and independent of age. Evolutionary biologist and data scientist Indre Zliobaite and her colleagues have observed a similar pattern in the evolutionary record of species. A common explanation of this apparent randomness is the "Red Queen Effect": if species are constantly fighting for survival in a changing environment with numerous competitors, extinction is a consistent possibility."

Another good resource is Jared Diamond, an expert who has written about these issues for many years. Diamond also includes relations with both friendly and hostile neighbors as critical variables .This is a link to one of Jared's TEDX talks.
https://www.ted.com/talks/jared_diamond_on_why_societies_colla pse?language=en#t-1079095

It's not just environmental issues that spur collapse it is also wealth inequity. Kemp calculates that the share of global wealth amongst the richest 1% has increased from around 25% in the 1980s to more than 40% in 2016.

Safa Motesharrei, at the University of Maryland, uses computer models to understand sustainability and collapse. Motesharrei and his colleagues say there are there are two key variables in the demise of a civilization: ecological strain and economic stratification.

"Disaster doesn't just come from the depletion of natural resources but also when the ruling class instigates instability and collapse by hoarding huge quantities of wealth and resources."

In a piece written by Rachel Nuwer summarizing the same issues

"Unfortunately, some experts believe such tough decisions exceed our political and psychological capabilities. "The world will not rise to the occasion of solving the climate problem during this century, simply because it is more expensive in the short term to solve the problem than it is to just keep acting as usual," says Jorgen Randers, a professor emeritus of climate strategy at the BI Norwegian Business School, and author of 2052: A Global Forecast for the Next Forty Years. "The climate problem will get worse and worse and worse because we won't be able to live up to what we've promised to do in the Paris Agreement and elsewhere."

"While we are all in this together, the world's poorest will feel the effects of collapse first. Indeed, some nations are already serving as canaries in the coal mine for the issues that may eventually pull apart more affluent ones. Syria, for example, enjoyed exceptionally high fertility rates for a time, which fueled rapid population growth. A severe drought in the late 2000s, likely made worse by human-induced climate change, combined with groundwater shortages to cripple agricultural production. That crisis left large numbers of people – especially young men – unemployed, discontent and desperate. Many flooded into urban centres, overwhelming limited resources and services there. Pre-existing ethnic tensions increased, creating fertile grounds for violence and conflict. On top of that, poor governance – including neoliberal policies that eliminated water subsidies in the middle of the drought – tipped the country into civil war in 2011 and sent it careening toward collapse."

Thomas Homer-Dixon, is chair of global systems at the Balsillie School of International Affairs in Waterloo, Canada, and author of *The Upside of Down.*

Rachel Nuwer writes:

"Homer-Dixon predicts that Western societies' collapse will be preceded by a retraction of people and resources back to their core homelands. As poorer nations continue to disintegrate amid conflicts and natural disasters, enormous waves of migrants will stream out of failing regions, seeking refuge in more stable states. Western societies will respond with restrictions and even bans on immigration; multi-billion dollar walls and border-patrolling drones and troops; heightened security on who and what gets in; and more authoritarian, populist styles of governing. "It's almost an immunological attempt by countries to sustain a periphery and push pressure back," Homer-Dixon says.

Nuwer goes on…
"Meanwhile, a widening gap between rich and poor within those already vulnerable Western nations will push society toward further instability from the inside. "By 2050, the US and UK will have evolved into two-class societies where a small elite lives a good life and there is declining well-being for the majority," Randers says. "What will collapse is equity."

Yet, complacency prevails, aided by the default human thinking style – cognitive bias.

Kemp issues a warning against complacency.

"…the world is worsening in areas that have contributed to the collapse of previous societies. The climate is changing, the gap between the rich and poor is widening, the world is becoming increasingly complex, and our demands on the environment are outstripping planetary carrying capacity."

"The collapse of our civilization is not inevitable. History suggests it is likely, but we have the unique advantage of being able to learn from the wreckages of societies past.

"We know what needs to be done: emissions can be reduced, inequalities levelled, environmental degradation reversed, innovation unleashed and economies diversified. The policy proposals are there. Only the political will is lacking. "

"We will only march into collapse if we advance blindly. We are only doomed if we are unwilling to listen to the past."

However, the cognitive biases and ways of thinking mentioned in this book aren't too comforting.

There is *temporal discounting* which shows that humans undervalue the future and overvalue the present and by the time they act it might well be too late.

There is the *Normalcy bias* which prevents us from accepting catastrophic change until it is upon us.

There is the *Illusion of control*, the tendency to overestimate our degree of influence over other external events.

Then there is the *optimism bias, the ostrich effect,* and the *overconfidence effect,* all of which lead to the underestimation of risk.

Then, of course, there's simple egotism. Will the rich and powerful face the reality that neglect of "ordinary people" will in the end be everyone's undoing?

Chapter Eighteen

The Evolution of Consciousness

Human consciousness has evolved over the centuries. According to Julian Jaynes, four thousand years ago, Man developed self-awareness and redefined his relationship with higher powers. Whereas, up to this point in time there were "gods" who were literally pulling the strings of their earthling puppets, now there was the concept of free will, which led to a redefinition of Man's relationship with a higher power. This was the beginning of monotheism, that there is one God, and he doesn't control us like the "Gods" used to, but rather encourages us to be virtuous.

What we now need, and pretty quickly, is the next evolution in consciousness, which allows us to rise above the limitations of the binary brain, simple stereotyping and the tyranny of the Lower Power. Without such an evolution, it is unlikely Man will survive. The simplistic brain encourages narcissism, and narcissism will keep us in our Lower Power, servants to greed, hatred and bigotry. And we have reached a point where there are certainly enough nuclear and biological weapons that sooner or later, the Lower Power will prevail and Mankind will go the way of the Dinosaur.

But how can we evolve? Is there any way of changing the brain?

Neuroplasticity

The brain does grow and adapt, sometimes in remarkable ways. Daniel Kish was blinded as a toddler but taught himself echolocation. Yes, he taught himself how to navigate through the world by using echoes to tell him where physical objects were. In case you think this is a fluke, Daniel has actually taught hundreds of others the same skill. When Daniel's brain was examined, the visual areas of the brain that are normally dormant in blind people, had made connections with the auditory area of the brain so that Daniel could literally "see" sounds. Is it possible we could create experiences that would change our abilities so we could focus on several things simultaneously, or minimize emotions so they don't become the driving force of our thoughts? Because our brains are limited, we don't know the answer to that question, but it certainly has some plausibility.

There are some people who do have a more rational brain and are much less persuaded by emotions and narratives. Of course, we sometimes call those people "weird" and "nerds" but might they be the blueprint, even the living manifestation, of the next evolution of consciousness? They are amongst the smartest and successful people precisely because they can modulate emotion, making them more capable of rational analysis. Sometimes these people are (mis)diagnosed as Asperger's syndrome, and like other diagnoses that is a complex label that cannot be accurately derived without a proper professional assessment. For example, Bill Gates, Steve Jobs and even Albert Einstein have been labeled with that diagnosis based on snippets of information and not on a complete assessment. I would expect that the most successful people would be those who are emotionally intelligent; they can understand and relate to other's feelings as well as their own AND they can manage theirs so that they can remain open-minded and have clarity and discernment.

Perhaps the emotionally intelligent will inherit the earth? Interestingly, I was recently reading a religious book, "Living the Gospel according to Matthew" by Father Ronald Rolheiser that helped me better understand the phrase, "the meek shall inherit the earth." What "the meek" meant here weren't wusses or the spineless. What "meek" meant were people who could control their emotions -- the emotionally intelligent. Let's hope that is so and the higher power prevails. If the lower power prevails there'll be no earth to inherit.

Now there are some people who are able to focus on a few things at the same time – and we call them crazy. There is a structure in the brain called the thalamus that filters out sensory information and sends just one input to consciousness for attention. But some people have a leaky thalamus and they get bombarded with several stimuli at the same time, which creates a conundrum. The brain has to make sense of the sensory input and as a result can become very creative at identifying patterns or indeed creating the connections between simultaneous stimuli. We call the people who have this problem "creative" -- when they are not being crazy. In fact, they straddle the line between being amazingly creative and out of their minds. There are many examples of such people in both the arts and sciences. John Nash, the mathematician with a beautiful mind, I believe fell into this category.

I have had several clients who were incredibly artistic and creative one day and psychotic the next. In fact, I once had a female client who was so brilliant the few weeks of the year that she could stay on the right side of the sanity line, that her company employed her *on an annual salary* for just those productive weeks because her output then was so amazing. The rest of the time, she was recovering or in psychosis. In short, her contract had a sanity clause -- although I do remember Harpo Marx in a Christmas related movie saying there was no such thing as Sanity Clause.

However, perhaps there is a way to develop the ability to see many different aspects of a situation at once and not have it overwhelm us. If we can't train the human brain to develop then we're left with other forms of intelligence to take on the mantle of protecting us from ourselves.

Artificial Intelligence

The other form of evolution will come in the form of artificial intelligence. While many people abhor the notion that rational, emotionless supercomputers might rule the world, it might not be a bad thing. Again, humans overvalue emotion because it's what drives us and it's what we know. But how bad would it be to have rational intelligence running things?

Here's a recent conversation with a friend of mine on this very topic.

Me: Do you know that one day soon, you'll be able to log in to something like RobotMD, enter your medical symptoms and get a complete logical breakdown of likely diagnoses and treatments. So, you have entered your medical history and the symptoms and within a few seconds Dr. Siri comes back with: "Based on all the information available there is a 75% chance your symptoms reflect X, a 44% chance they reflect Y and a 15% chance they reflect Z and a 3% chance it is a combination of the above. If you follow this treatment regimen there is an 89% chance of recovery within 3 days."

Friend: That's terrible! I want to talk to a real person.

Me: Even if they are less accurate?

Friend: Yep, no one will ever accept that sort of medical treatment.

Me: They said that about books, remember. No one will want to read a digital device, they'll always want to hold a real book?

Friend: Well, this is different. This is your health.

Me: Which is why you would want it to be as accurate as possible.

Friend: I would never subscribe to that system.

Me: Even, if it were more accurate at diagnosis and treatment?

Friend: Never

Me: You could log on any time of the day or night from anywhere. Instant treatment.

Friend: No way
Me: Just $18 a "visit."

Friend: Where can I sign up?

Me: Well all of that will be old news in a couple of years. How about 10 years into the future?

Friend: I was just getting used to the idea of Dr. Siri.

Me: Well, she'll still be around. You will have a variety of internal and external sensors that will be monitoring your physical state and, of course, matched to your medical history. When something's awry, Siri will alert you and tell you there's a problem.

Friend: Then I go online and visit RobotMD, right?

Me: Not necessary. Siri has already worked out the problem and ordered your medications, which will arrive via drone within the hour.

Friend: So, no need for doctors then?

Me: Maybe they might assist the robot in surgery.

Friend: Yes, I have heard about the da Vinci surgical robot.

Me: Yes, it's here already. Imagine what it will be doing in a decade.

But do we need artificial intelligence? What about the best forms of human intelligence? Doesn't science provide us with an enhanced intelligence that can be used? Can the scientific process guide our thought process?

Aliens

In addition to the evolution of consciousness, there's the possibility before there's much more human evolution, creatures from a distinct galaxy will reach us and train us to be as smart as they are. However, a word of caution.

Cattle have about an 80% genetic similarity to humans and chickens are about 60% similar. Now suppose that this alien life form has evolved genetically and we have about 80% of their genes. That would make them see us like we see cattle. Then, there would be a good chance that rather than evolving we would be mined for the famous intergalactic restaurant chain MacSpock and all be turned into SpockBurgers.

Only time will tell.

Conclusion

The implication is that in human affairs, we fool ourselves into thinking we have rationality on our side when many of us don't have the capacity to know what is logical and what isn't. We need to understand the process of thinking and the inherent biases to have insight at all into our – or anyone else's – thought process..

The *decisions* we make are often what Kahneman calls "fast and frugal." They are based on emotion and intuition with a cursory nod in the direction of logic. The fact of the matter, however, is that if you want to believe something, no amount of logical argument is going to get in your way. If human beings are anything we are great rationalizers, which, of course, is different from being rational.

It is an advance that there are now books addressing these critical issues and looking at how the flawed thinking process plays out in different areas of society and life. Make no mistake, every area of life, from medicine to law, from politics to everything, is impacted by cognitive bias.

How to Think Like a Sage
The key to intelligent decisions is therefore, to understand how the mind works and distorts perception, hijacks memory and creates emotion. By understanding these processes and the key biases that result from it, you can at least be aware of the potential pitfalls in thinking and decision-making. Now many people purport to tell you how to think. Often these are books are about self-limiting beliefs and how to change them. However, many of these books are really about *what to think* not *how to think*.

Unquestionably, technology will expose us to more and more information and also be able to do more for us. But I'm not sure that either of those developments will allow us to evolve beyond story-telling rationalizers. In fact, they might make the problem worse by making us lazy and overwhelming us with even more information, distracting us and training us to lose our focus.

Earlier I mentioned the research on numeracy and literacy. Devices to answer numerical problems have been around quite a while and might give us some insight into how the reliance on technology can either help or hinder our evolution.

Adrienne Bernhard writes:

"While mathematical illiteracy makes life hard for individuals, its consequences are truly global: research suggests a correlation between poor numeracy skills and national unemployment, productivity, even physical health. But does it really matter if we cannot think quantitatively when we have phones and other devices that can do it for us?"

"The population now falsely assumes you can calculate everything, because of technology," says Conrad Wolfram, Strategic director of Wolfram Europe. From exam results to fake-news, "things that have a number attached to them are sometimes used beyond their ability to judge."

"We will always need solid numeracy habits in order to make the most of the technology we use. Even the most sophisticated artificial intelligence machines are only as good as the data they are trained on, and human involvement, whether purposeful or accidental, can muddy that data."

The safeguard against this abdication of a fundamental skill like numeracy include…

- Resist the temptation to rely on devices to work numerical problems

- Take the context into account

- Use computers wisely

- Be skeptical

This advice is applicable to all cognitive skills, not just numeracy.

On the other hand, technology might help by training us to be able to focus productively on more than one thing at a time and thus changing the brain. But first things first – we need to be made more aware how we really think.

What do you need?
Awareness of the thinking process. Without understanding of the default settings of the human brain you will not be able to assess your or other's thought processes. It's important to understand the common flaws and biases.

Emotion control. Because emotion drives the narrative, you need to manage your emotions, otherwise they will certainly control you.

Logic training. It's important to grasp the fundamentals of logical analysis, including some statistics and the understanding of "research."

Spiritual training. To truly think like a genius, you need to get outside of your own ego and adopt the practice of the adaptive defensive mechanisms that are also the cornerstone of an authentic life.

And, finally….

I want to thank you for your valuable time and attention in reading this book. A book is nothing without a reader. You have got to know me a little and made my effort in writing the book worthwhile. Regardless of what you think of the book, I appreciate your effort in trying to understand what I am attempting to convey.

Now, as you have invested in me, I feel it only right and fair to tell you a bit more about me. I want you to hear from it me. I want to tell you. I need to tell you in the interests of the integrity of our relationship.

I was a successful psychologist for many years. I started out in the UK working in addictions at a time when psychologists were beginning to enter the field. From then I have worked in a number of capacities and organizations. I have been a researcher and academic, writing more than 30 scientific articles. I have run inpatient and outpatient eating disorders programs, addiction programs, and held teaching jobs at major universities. I had been involved in projects with the World Health Organization and The National Institute of Health. When I came to the US thirty years ago, I was the director of a leading residential health and wellness program, and have also given thousands of talks, as well as being a consultant to major health groups like Take Off Pounds Sensibly (TOPS).

In 2010 I started to integrate neuroscience and neuro-technology into my practice and conducted one of the first projects in the US public school system using EEG brain mapping with troubled elementary school children in the Independence, Missouri School District. I was also beginning to work with the military using neuro-technology in different settings. My work has been featured in many media outlets and I have appeared on CNN, ABC's 20/20 and The View. At that point I had also written 10 books in my own name as well as co-written another four, mostly in the areas of health and wellness. My main goal in life has always been to help others.

All of that fell apart in 2012.

I had always been respectful of my clients' boundaries, even though a few were them weren't respectful of mine. In 2005, I took on a difficult case, a female Borderline Personality Disorder who was highly seductive. There was an ever-present sexual undertone from her that I was constantly deflecting. There were even overt messages about having sex, which I declined, reminding her that this was not the purpose of therapy or my intention.

You can see where this is going.

In 2008, she quit therapy which I was happy to approve because it was getting too much. I referred her on to other therapists. A few months later she asked if she could come and see me and I agreed for her to visit me but not as therapy. She agreed. She worked close by as a valued employee in a real estate team as well as doing some side work in the tech field. She dropped by periodically for four years. During that time, I started the integration of neuroscience into my practice and I asked a variety of people I knew who were not clients, to participate in the trial phase of testing equipment and testing. She participated in that, scoring very highly on cognitive tests.

My purpose in these periodic visits was to show to her that she could have a friendship with a guy that wasn't sexual.

It was a bad idea, in retrospect, although it worked for four years.

One day in late July 2012, after a brief visit she kissed me. For a couple of days, it was all downhill from there and we had a very brief, consensual sexual encounter. Then I stopped it. I was trapped in the moment and *temporal discounting* came to the fore and would permanently change my life.

About a month later, I got a call from the SC Licensing Board telling me that someone had made a complaint against me for sexual misconduct. My attorney told me that my best strategy was to plead for mercy and not challenge any testimony. To cut a very long story short, six months later the Board voted to permanently revoke my license.

I have never seen the investigator's report. As I was writing this book, I reached out again and requested a copy, through the Freedom of Information Act. My request was denied. So, I have been denied the narrative that the Board members were working off.

I don't know what happened. I don't know what the former client told them, or who else testified and why. But at least I tried to find out. And I can only tell you my experience. I'm sure it is biased but then again, I'm also sure the Board members narrative was biased, too.

And so I'm a testament to one of the main messages of the book…

There's no such thing as objectivity. You have just got to get as close to it as you can.

I have spent the last several years soul searching and working hard to restore trust and respect. I have several roles in the community including bringing brain health via the national Healthy Minds Initiative, a non-profit of which I am a Board member. I healed my relationship with my wife and started out on a journey of exploration that led me to this book. My purpose remains to help others and I have found a way to do that through my writing and more recently, coaching and consulting. Interestingly, I had always wanted to be a writer growing up but veered into psychology instead as it seemed to offer a more rewarding future.

Thank you for listening -- and reading.

You can't ask any more from someone that they listen to you with respect

How Not to Think

Workbook

Hopefully, you now have a better understanding of the factors that influence the thinking process and how the mind's default setting can lead us into bias that blind us to the reality of our situations.

In the text I have already hinted at how we can become more rational and develop critical thinking. In this section I will provide some practical tools that will help you become more balanced and open-minded, as well as understanding.

How not to think refers to two processes:
1. Turning off the processing activity in the brain so you can take a different perspective and reach a different level of consciousness,
2. Identifying and avoiding cognitive biases, false assumptions, and lack of logic

Step 1: Understand the thought process
If you have read through I Think Therefore I Am Wrong you will now have insight into several important details. Specifically…

- Memory can be unreliable

- Unconscious processes can direct our emotions, perceptions and thoughts

- Environmental influences, including other people, influence our memory and perception

- We are more interested in emotional comfort and consistency than "the truth"

- We use defenses and cognitive biases to justify our positions

- We typically engage in binary thinking that seriously limits critical thinking

- The media and advertisers have mastered the art of manipulation

Wisdom is understanding these influences on our mental processes and adapting accordingly.

All behavior change begins with awareness, but awareness itself is not enough. We need to act differently to think differently.

The tools in this workbook include techniques to manage emotions, identify and challenge assumptions, recognize and neutralize cognitive biases, adapting spiritual values and developing a healthy lifestyle.

Programming Self
We are programing our minds and brains every second of the day through the things we think and do. Remember the brain will do and learn what you train it to do. To learn new ways of doing anything, including thinking, we have to act differently. When we do, we create new connections in our brains that provide the infrastructure for new behavior. We literally are changing our brains.

You have read about the *availability bias* which shows that we are overly influenced by what we focus on. So, your focus on this change process needs to be really emphasized to your brain through specific actions like journaling, meditation and other mindfulness tools.

Emotional Control

One of the keys to effective and objective thinking is the management of emotions. As you have read, emotion often drives the narrative, especially when it is ramped up.

It's not that emotions are negative. Sure, some of them can make us feel uncomfortable, but they are valuable signs and indicators about what is going in our interaction with the world. They need to be listened to, decoded and then lead to conscious and considered action to address the issues they have exposed.

Let's look at your emotions.

How common are these emotions in your life. Rank them from1 to 5, where 1= hardly ever, 2= not very often, 3=sometimes, 4= frequently and 5= very frequently.

Anger_____
Anxiety_____
Depression_____
Frustration_____
Guilt_____
Joy _____

How well do you think you manage your emotions?
Rank them from1 to 5, where 1= poorly, 2= not very well, 3=ok, 4= fairly well and 5= great.

Anger_____
Anxiety_____
Depression_____
Frustration_____
Guilt_____
Joy_____

What methods do you use to manage uncomfortable emotions?
Check the methods you use on a regular basis

- Physical exercise
- Yoga, Qi Gong, Tai Chi
- Meditation and Mindfulness practice
- Talking with others
- Drinking alcohol
- Using prescribed or OTC medications
- Using street drugs
- Eating high sugar foods

Let's consider the effective methods of emotion management.

1. Physical activity
Physical exercise is arguably the best emotion manager.
For decades now, practitioners have realized the value of
physical activity as a great tool for managing anxiety and
depression.

Physical activity increases the neurotransmitters in the
brain associated with energy, motivation and well-being. It
also takes you out of processing mode and puts you into a
different mental state. It also uses energy and changes your
focus. All of these benefits combine to reduce your
emotional arousal.

There are many purposes of physical activity, for example,
increase strength, and provide a cardiovascular workout.

Cardiovascular physical activity that can help with
emotion management can vary depending on your level of
fitness. As a rule…

- Any physical activity is better than none at all

- The longer the better
- The more intense (relative to your own level of fitness) the better.

There are advantages of activity at different times of the day. An early morning workout can energize you for the day. A mid-afternoon workout can prevent the typical drop of energy that occurs in the mid-afternoon hours.

Any physical activity is better than none, so even if all you can manage is a 15 minute walk, go for it. Don't forget though, that longer and more strenuous the better the effect.

The environment where you can exercise can also add to the benefits. For example, if you are walking, running or biking in nature, the environment will help you relax and can often improve your perspective.

Try to do some physical activity every day, but specifically use it when you are feeling overwhelmed by an uncomfortable emotion. If it helps, try to exercise with a friend to get added accountability and support.

Write down the names of people you could exercise with:

_____
_____
_____
_____
_____
_____

Write down the cardiovascular activities that you will do. These could include: Walking, jogging, running, swimming, biking

I am going to use the following activities to control by mind and consciousness

---

Resistance exercises can also be beneficial to managing your consciousness. The benefits of increasing your strength and the feeling of committing yourself to enhancing your body and self can be powerful.

There are many different forms of resistance exercise, from simple lifting of weights to more complex activities on specific equipment like rowing machines. At the very least you can get some weights and spend just a few minutes three times a week going through a series of core exercises.

Physical activity as described above is essential for not just emotion management but a healthy mind and body. It should be a foremost priority in your life.

I am going to do the following resistance exercises

---

2. Energetic techniques
Many of the physical techniques from Eastern traditions are based on the notion of releasing energy and increasing its flow around the body. These exercises can be very helpful in getting centered and managing emotions. The conscious control of your body is often accompanied by a similar sense of control of your mind, which is what we're after here.

Yoga:
According to various sources, yoga has three effects that are relevant to wisdom and the expansion of consciousness.

1. A meditative means of discovering dysfunctional perception and cognition, as well as overcoming it for release from suffering, inner peace and salvation;
2. The raising and expansion of consciousness from oneself to being coextensive with everyone and everything:
3. A path to omniscience and enlightened consciousness enabling one to comprehend the impermanent (illusive, delusive) and permanent (true, transcendent) reality.

Qi Gong:
Qigong practice typically involves moving meditation, coordinating slow-flowing movement, deep rhythmic breathing, and a calm meditative state of mind. People practice qigong throughout China and worldwide for recreation, exercise, relaxation, preventive medicine, self-healing, alternative medicine, meditation, self-cultivation, and training for martial arts.

Tai Chi:
Tai Chi is also an energetic practice with elements of martial arts training and meditation.

(Ref: Tai Chi and Qi Gong: In Depth". National Center for Complementary and Integrative Health, US National Institutes of Health. October 2016.)

Which of the above techniques are you going to explore?

3. Meditation and Mindfulness

There are many different forms of meditation but almost all of them are designed to change the level of consciousness and focus.

When we are concentrating and are in processing mode, we are typically focused on input in a very specific way. For example, we might be trying to write a report or listen to a talk. In this mode we are in Beta wave processing mode.

There are broadly 4 different types of brain waves that cover most mental activity.

Beta: 13-30 cycles per second (cpc). Processing mode, focused concentration

Alpha: 8-13 cpc. Relaxed wakefulness

Theta: 4-8 cpc. Light sleep or deep meditation.

Delta: 1-4 cpc. Deeper sleep.

We need to spend time in the Alpha and Theta states. That's time to reflect, but perhaps more importantly time to experience. Rather than imposing a frame of reference on consciousness (top-down processing), we simply experience it as it comes to us (bottom-up processing). This allows us to step out of habitual experience and open ourselves up to new possibilities and insights.

In excess, Beta processing mode is associated with anxiety, obsessions and even delusions. Clearly, we can become overwhelmed when we stay in that brain state.

Meditation practices in the broad sense of the word are designed to reach a different state of awareness. Often used with deep breathing exercises, these techniques allow control over the nervous system, thus critically reducing emotion and enabling us to step outside our normal and habitual physiological and psychological reactions.

Evidence suggests that experienced meditators develop more compassion and even change the structures in their brains associated with emotional processing.

The ability to develop an objectivity about your thoughts and emotions is key to the development of the values mentioned in the book.

Remember the story of the student observing his master laughing at his anger?

This distance from habitual response, assumptions and thoughts is a key to mindfulness and consciousness.

When you can reach this level of awareness you are freed from reflexive responses and can live truly in the moment with much greater insight and wisdom.

Here's a simple meditation exercise that includes several rules for such exercises in general.

Find a comfortable space where you will not be interrupted by any noise. If necessary, disconnect phones and turn off any devices.

Find a comfortable spot. Sit with your feet, waist, shoulders and neck, aligned. Your head should be facing straight ahead, not dropping or pointing up.

Slowly breathe in through your nose. When you exhale, breathe out slowly through your nose. Deep breathing is key and is a useful exercise on its own as it calms the nervous system, minimizing or even eliminating emotional arousal.

Start your deep breathing. When you're ready, imagine yourself sitting on a river bank. A river flows from left to right across your imagination. As a thought enters your mind, watch it flow down the river and eventually out of sight. Just observe it. Do not analyze it or even try to remember it, just watch it.

Here's another simple exercise for sensory information.

Get into the meditation position and start deep breathing. Then put all your focus into your ears. Just put all your attention in listening to any sounds you can hear. Just experience them. Don't try to judge them, guess where they are coming from or remember them.

An adaptation of the above exercise is to choose a food. As you are eating it, close your eyes and just pay attention to the taste and feel of food in your mouth. What is that experience?

These exercises are practice in ways of focusing your consciousness and stepping outside of automatic top-down processing. The goal is to develop this skill and then use it at important times of your life. Meditation exercises are not just about developing the skill by practicing daily, but actually using it in "real life".

For more information and access to different types of mindfulness exercises please visit www.mindfulnessexercises.com

Cognitive Biases
There are some simple exercises that can help you identify and put a check on most cognitive biases. Here are some tools for the leading biases.

Availability Bias
Recognize that you are going to be overly influenced by the information that is available to you.

1. How reliable is the information you are basing your perception on?

2. What other information do you ideally need to be convinced your perception is valid?

3. Is there other information that contradicts your perception?

4. If there's other information, what is it?

_____

_____

_____

_____

_____

_____

_____

_____

_____

_____

_____

Anchoring Bias

We can get caught in unconsciously anchoring our thoughts about a particular topic.

1. What assumptions are anchoring your thinking about this issue?
2. Why are they anchoring your thoughts?
3. How do these anchors limit your thought process?
4. How could you reframe the anchors?
5. How could you have no anchors to your perception?

_____
_____
_____
_____
_____
_____

Confirmation Bias

We continually look for information that supports our views and dismiss information that doesn't.

1. Seek out disconfirming information
2. Study it.
3. Pretend that you agree with it, and write down the reasons why
4. What are the faults in the confirming information? Write these down

_____
_____
_____
_____

_____

_____

Temporal discounting

We discount the future and often don't plan accordingly.

1. Imagine your life ten years from now. Write down what it looks like.

_____

_____

_____

_____

_____

_____

2. Imagine your life twenty years from now. Write down what it looks like.

_____

_____

_____

_____

_____

3. Imagine your life thirty years from now. Write down what it looks like.

_____

_____

_____

_____

_____

Download the agingbooth app from
https://apps.apple.com/us/app/agingbooth/id357467791 or
similar app.

Advance the app so you're ten years older. Repeat
question 1.

_____

_____

_____

_____

_____

_____

Advance the app so you're twenty years older. Repeat
question 2

_____

_____

_____

_____

_____

_____

Advance the app so you're thirty years older. Repeat
question 3.

_____

_____

_____

_____

_____

_____

Framing Effect

The way information is presented to you, will affect your perception. So, identifying how it is presented and asking yourself questions about why it is presented that way can lead to a more balanced view.

1. How is this material being presented?
2. Why is it being presented the way it is?
3. What is the intention of the presentation of material?
4. How could the material be presented differently?
5. What effect would a different presentation have on your perception?

_____
_____
_____
_____
_____
_____

Facts or probabilities

Often material is presented as factual when it is effectively a probability.

1. Is someone claiming that a statement they make is 100% true?
2. Is it 100% true or merely a probability? For example, is it 100% true that everyone loses weight on this program, or is that just some people do? And

if so, what percentage lose what amount of weight and how long is the weight loss maintained?

3. How do presented "facts" compare to what is known about the general data in the field? For example, what are the data on maintained weight loss over a period of time, e.g. two years. Is the statement consistent with the known data?

4. How are the "data" collected on which statements of fact are based?

_____

_____

_____

_____

_____

_____

_____

_____

_____

_____

_____

_____

Halo Effect

Often we can exaggerate someone's qualities because we like them and we know they have strengths.

1. What do you think about this person's qualities such as intelligence, sociability, communication skills, appearance, and values?

2. Are all these qualities judged equally favorably?

3. What is the evidence for your perception for each of these imputed skills?

_____

_____

_____

_____

_____

_____

_____

_____

_____

_____

_____

Gossip

When you hear gossip about someone ask yourself these questions.

1. How true is the gossip?
2. What is the agenda of the people spreading the gossip?
3. If this was being said about you, how would you feel?
4. What would you hope people would do before spreading gossip about you?

_____

_____

_____

_____

_____

I don't know

Assumptions and biases exist because we don't like to admit we don't know. However, one of the keys to wisdom is to recognize that we don't know. We don't have to have the answer to everything. It's okay to say, "I don't know".

Now write out fifty times, "I don't know".

_____
_____
_____
_____
_____
_____

_____
_____
_____
_____
_____
_____

_____
_____
_____
_____
_____

Spirituality, Integrity and Values.

The book shows the connection between values and more balanced perspectives, thinking and actions.

Acceptance

You have a choice. Dealing with the issue is by far better than ignoring it or denying it.

1. Do you typically accept your situation or try to ignore it?
2. How does your strategy affect your thinking?
3. Are you going to accept your situation and face up to it? Why?

_____

_____

_____

_____

_____

_____

_____

_____

_____

_____

_____

_____

_____

_____

_____

_____

_____

Altruism

Helping others is a great way to get outside of yourself and find a different perspective. Opportunities abound every day to help others, from single acts of kindness to more organized charitable activities.

1. What activities do you do?
2. What activities could you do?
3. How does an altruistic mindset affect your thinking?
4. Where can you find out about altruistic opportunities in your area?

_____
_____
_____
_____
_____
_____
_____

_____
_____
_____
_____
_____
_____

_____
_____
_____
_____
_____
_____

Compassion

Interdependence is key. If we want the support of others, then we need to be prepared to also walk in their shoes.

Compassion isn't just being empathic and understanding what someone is experiencing, it also involves empowering them to deal with their stuff.

1. How can you express your compassion?
2. Do you show compassion in your relationships?
3. How does your compassion, or lack thereof, affect your thinking?
4. Could you do more?
5. If so, what?

_____
_____
_____
_____
_____
_____
_____

_____
_____
_____
_____
_____
_____

_____
_____
_____
_____
_____

Courage
Don't live in fear. Fear stands for **F**alse **E**xpectations **A**ppearing **R**eal.

1. What are you not being courageous about?
2. How does your level of courage affect your thought process?
3. How could you find more courage?
4. Who could help you be more courageous?

_____

_____

_____

_____

_____

_____

_____

_____

_____

_____

_____

_____

_____

_____

_____

_____

_____

Forgiveness
Forgiveness is about forgiving yourself as much as others. It's not about condoning or not agreeing with an action, it's about moving on.

1. What do you have to forgive yourself for?
2. How will you forgive yourself?
3. How does forgiveness affect your thinking?

4. Who do you need to forgive?
5. When are you going to do that?

_____
_____
_____
_____
_____
_____
_____

_____
_____
_____
_____
_____
_____

_____
_____
_____
_____
_____
_____

Gratitude

If you're not grateful for what you have, you're always be dissatisfied.

1. What are the things that you grateful for?
2. Why are you grateful for them?
3. How does your gratitude affect your thinking?
4. When are you going to be grateful for those things every day?

_____
_____
_____
_____
_____
_____

_____
_____
_____
_____
_____
_____

_____
_____
_____
_____
_____

Honesty
You can't have self-respect if you're a liar and deceive yourself as well as others.

1. Have you ever been dishonest? Write down the situations.
2. Have you ever been honest when it would have been easier to lie? If so, how did it feel?
3. How does your level of honesty affect your thinking?
4. How do you feel about people who are dishonest with you?
5. Make a commitment to never lie again.

_____
_____
_____
_____
_____
_____
_____

_____
_____
_____
_____
_____
_____
_____

_____
_____
_____
_____
_____
_____

Humility
Don't get too full of yourself. Practice interdependence and develop your strengths.

1. Do you see yourself as humble?
2. Do you think others see you as humble?
3. How does your humility affect your thinking?
4. What makes people view others as egocentric?
5. How could you practice humility?

_____
_____

_____

_____

_____

_____

_____

_____

_____

_____

_____

_____

_____

_____

_____

_____

_____

_____

Humor

Don't take yourself too seriously. See the funny side of things.

1. How could you introduce more humor into your life?
2. Who do you/could you hang out with, who makes you laugh?
3. How would more humor affect your thinking?
4. Could you read more humorous stuff and read funny material? How and when?

_____

_____

_____

_____

_____

_____

_____

_____

_____

_____

_____

_____

_____

_____

_____

_____

_____

Mercy
Practicing mercy on yourself then others. Give yourself a
break. Recognize we are all imperfect, but we all have
strengths.

1. What are your strengths?
2. In what ways do you need to give yourself a break?
3. In what ways do you need to give others a break?
4. How would being more merciful affect your
   thinking?
5. Who do you need to be more merciful to?

_____

_____

_____

_____

_____
_____
_____
_____
_____
_____
_____
_____
_____
_____
_____
_____

Moderation

Be moderate in all things.

1. What are your excessive behaviors?
2. How could you moderate them?
3. How do your excessive behaviors affect you?
4. How would more moderation affect your thinking?

_____
_____
_____
_____
_____
_____
_____

_____
_____
_____
_____

_____
_____
_____
_____
_____
_____

Patience

Patience is important for emotional control and thus wisdom.

1. Are you a patient person?
2. In what situations are you impatient?
3. How would more patience affect your thinking?
4. How could you improve your patience?

_____
_____
_____
_____
_____

_____
_____
_____
_____
_____

_____

_____

_____

_____

_____

_____

Respect
Have respect for yourself and others. People are imperfect but that doesn't mean you should disrespect them.

1. Do you respect yourself?
2. In what ways do you disrespect yourself?
3. Who do you respect?
4. Who don't you respect?
5. How would being more respectful influence your thinking?
6. How could you improve your respectfulness?

_____

_____

_____

_____

_____

_____

_____

_____

_____

_____

_____

_____

_____

_____
_____
_____
_____

Tolerance

Tolerance is an important aspect of wisdom. Remember many times, you don't know.

1. Are you a tolerant person?
2. How does your intolerance affect your thinking?
3. How could you improve your tolerance?

_____
_____
_____
_____
_____

_____
_____
_____
_____
_____
_____

_____
_____
_____
_____
_____
_____

Work

Commit yourself to improving the values mentioned in this section.

1. In what ways are you going to commit to developing these values?
2. How will improving these values affect your thinking?
3. Where will this work stand in relation to your priorities?

_____
_____
_____
_____
_____
_____

_____
_____
_____
_____
_____
_____
_____
_____
_____
_____

Courses in Critical Thinking

Finally, I encourage you to consider taking a critical thinking course. Many of these available.

For further insight I am directing to you here:
https://digitaldefynd.com/best-critical-thinking-courses/

This site reviews the five best critical thinking courses available.

Acknowledgements

Thank you to my beautiful wife, MJ whose compassion and understanding have helped me immeasurably. Thank you, darling, for your patience as I worked on this book.

Thank you, too, to my amazing son James for being such an inspiration and giving my life so much meaning.

Thanks, also, to my wonderful mother-in-law Ellen whose support and compassion are inspirational.

Thanks to Josh, my autistic son, for teaching me so much.

Special thanks, too, to my dog Jack for faithfully sitting by me many times, while I was writing this.

About Howard Rankin

Howard has to date written 12 books in his own name, co-authored another 8 and ghostwritten 30 others.

Howard is also a Health Coach, Consultant and Speaker on Communication, Cognitive Bias and Brain Health Initiatives. Please visit his coaching page at www.drhowardjrankin.com

He is an Associate at Meraki Warrior, a business strategy and consulting company.

He hosts the podcast How Not To Think that is available on Buzzsprout and many other platforms.

Howard serves as a Board member and director on Dean and Ayesha Sherzai's non-profit Healthy Minds Initiative, and Pax Bonum, a Catholic charity.

Howard can be reached at DrHRankin@gmail.com.

References

Airely, D. (2010) Predictably Irrational: The Hidden Forces that Shape Our Decisions. Harper.

Diamond, J (2011) Collapse: How Societies Choose to Fail or Succeed (2nd edition) Penguin

Kahneman, D. (2013) Thinking, Fast and Slow. Farrar, Straus and Giroux

Macknick, S and Martinez-Conde, S (with Blakely S.) (2010) Sleights of Mind. What the Neuroscience of Magic Reveals about Our Everyday Deceptions. Picador.

Damasio, A. (1994) Descartes Error: Emotion, Reason and the Human Brain. Putnam

Benforado, A. (2015) Unfair: The New Science of Criminal Injustice, Crown.

Ratey, J with Hagerman, E. (2008) Spark: The Revolutionary New Science of Exercise and The Brain. Little, Brown and Co.

Sherzai, Dean and Ayesha: (2017) The Alzheimer's Solution. Harper One.

Rolheiser, R (1999) The Holy Longing: The Search for a Christian Spirituality. Image

Barry, D. (1996) Dave Barry's Complete Guide to Guys. Ballantine.

Barrett, L. (2018) How Emotions Are Made. Houghton, Mifflin Harcourt.

A selection of other recent books by Howard Rankin

Power Talk: The Art of Effective Communication, 2rd edition

Inspired to Lose

10 Steps to a Great Relationship

Beyond the Comfort Zone: The Complete Guide to Authentic Management (with John Jacobs).

Breaking the Press: The Incredible Story of the All American Red Heads. (with Orwell Moore and Tammy Harrison Moore)

In God's Waiting Room (with Barbara Morello-O'Donnell)

Finding Happiness (with Todd Patkin)

7 Steps to Wellness

Weight Loss Interviews